CANADIAN SPORTFISHING

Henry Waszczuk 🍁 *Italo Labignan*

"The science of fishing can be had from books; the art is learned by the catching and losing of fish." W.H. Blake, Brown Waters, 1915.

ISBN 0-9692391-0-6

Front cover by Hills Video

1986 Canadian Sportfishing Promotions
P.O. Box 84 Carlisle, Ontario

ACKNOWLEDGEMENTS

Over the years, both of us have gained a great deal of fishing knowledge from our experiences with our fathers, guides, charter boat captains as well as various other anglers, both amateur and pro.

The following tips, techniques and helpful hints are made possible by the generosity and sportsmanship of fellow anglers. We extend our thanks also to those fishermen who have gone un-named, but have contributed to this material.

Many thanks to Sheilagh Mercer for her excellent sketches and to the corporate members of the fishing and boating industry who helped support our project.

Special thanks also goes to our families for bearing with our absence and our long hours at the desk tabulating this information so that we all can be more successful sportfishermen.

Foreword

All editors are skeptical by nature and those who edit fishing stories and articles become exceedingly so. When I was approached by the authors of this handbook to write a foreword I was reluctant to accept the invitation. My first thoughts were that another book on fishing would only add to the proliferation of such books being presently marketed. The shelves in my library are already groaning under the weight of books dealing with angling. This is not surprising when it is considered that man has gone after fish since well before the beginning of recorded history.

I first met Henry Waszczuk and Italo Labignan while acting as one of the officials at one of the Labatt Fishing Series. In tournaments that followed I noted that they were frequently among the prize winners. Recently I edited some of their articles for the Angler and Hunter magazine and became more aware of their knowledge relating to sportfishing and recreational angling. This knowledge is revealed on the following pages and I'm sure that application of the many tips and techniques will result in more fish for readers of this handbook.

Good luck and tight lines!

Jack Davis

Jack Davis

Introduction

Piscator Non Solum Piscatur – "It is not all of fishing to fish". Motto of a storied fraternity of Kawartha Lakes musky men, those words of wisdom are worth remembering.

Fishing is a multi-faceted flexible recreation that's easily plied to suit oneself.

It can revitalize or relax, be competitive or contemplative. Some prefer to make it a solitary pursuit and to others, angling is synonymous with companionship and camaraderie.

Many find that fishing is a safety valve on the pressure cooker in which they live and work.

While those who crave action can find it in abundance, conversely, angling is also tailored for trophy hunters – eternal optimists who thrive on the challenge and possess the patience of Job. Although brimming with enthusiasm and anticipation, they don't really expect to hook a wall-hanger every trip or, for that matter, every year. Hope springs eternal, however, and they're content with an outside chance.

Fishing should be fun and reigns supreme as a font for tall tales that sometimes transcend the boundaries of believability.

Some fish stories are good for a lifetime of laughs, bringing to mind the time co-author Henry Waszczuk bagged the biggest salmon in a major tournament. Unfortunately, having overlooked the rule which stated the catch had to be kept until after the final whistle in order to qualify for the prize, Henry swallowed the evidence!

Angling sweeps aside society's status symbols. Worldly wealth or a lofty position doesn't make a person a better fisherman than someone on the bottom rung with nought to his name.

Fishing bridges the generation gap, being something youngsters and oldsters can enjoy together.

The father who doesn't introduce his progeny to worm dunking is shirking his parental responsibilities, cheating his kids and short-changing himself, to boot.

Rewards include the joy of watching an excited boy or girl fight a fish. Any fish. Size and species are irrelevant to smallfry.

You've done a good job when it's time to leave for home and a little voice pleads: "Can I please have one more last cast?"

The professor can be justifiably proud when his pupil releases a fish without any prompting. Putting back fish not destined for immediate consumption demonstrates sportsmanship, maturity and a conservation conscience.

Same as singing, you don't have to be gifted to enjoy it, but it helps if you know the tune. More knowledge means more enjoyment.

This treatise of top-notch tips from top-flight fishermen will expand know-how and hone angling skills.

Read, absorb, enjoy!

John Power

About the Authors

Both Henry Waszczuk and Italo Labignan are well-known sportfishing personalities, writers and fishing educators. Each year, they travel throughout the province of Ontario with mini-sportfishing shows reaching both the young and old with successful fishing techniques and products. Professionally, they have consistently placed well among the best pro fishermen on the tournament scene.

Their handbook is an illustrated masterpiece of over 1000 fishing tips, hints and techniques. The angler will be able to clearly and easily learn how to catch more fish, saving valuable fishing time and money. First in a series, this angling classic will indeed be a welcome to everyone's home library.

Table of Contents

Fellow Angler:

Throughout Canada, sporting associations give the angler a much needed and much heeded voice in the issues that affect you. In Ontario, the Federation of Anglers and Hunters is just that.

For 58 years the O.F.A.H., Ontario's largest provincial conservation association, has been democratically representing the views of its member sportsmen, ensuring that Ontario's fish and wildlife resources are managed wisely. Like you, Italo and I realize the size of the job ahead if Ontario's good fishing is to be maintained and poor fishing improved. As strong and professional as the O.F.A.H. is, an eye to the future tells us that it's membership must grow to meet the increasingly complex challenges to our sport: acid rain, industrial pollution, poaching, wetland drainage and loss of habitat, the use of gill nets by the commercial fishing industry, deteriorating water quality, water diversions, the use of fish by Ontario's native peoples, and so on.

As anglers, we all want to see lots of healthy game fish spawning in clean waters wherever we go in this beautiful province. We urge you to join us in supporting the Ontario Federation of Anglers and Hunters with a membership. Your sport depends on it!

Henry Waszczuk

General Fishing Tips

General Fishing Tips

Freshwater fishing continues to be one of Canada's number one growing outdoor activities. Being relatively inexpensive, sportfishing can seemingly give a limitless number of enjoyable hours throughout our Canadian provinces.

A good quality rod and reel and a supply of artifical lures may cost as little as $75.00. Numerous fishing camps provide boat rentals, general fishing information, even guides for those anglers not familiar with the area.

The sport of fishing has so many facets, from different types of equipment to the variety of fish you can catch under all types of conditions. Over the years, anglers have found that by doing certain things a certain way, they can enjoy fishing more by catching more fish in a shorter period of time. Although fishing from a boat would be preferable, fishing from banks or from a wading position is often as productive when angling for the large variety of available gamefish.

For example, Ontario sports more than a dozen different types of fish that offer considerable challenges to the angler. Bass, pike, muskie, and many salmonoid species are very popular, but the favourite gamefish in many of the provinces is still "walleye".

In all due respect, your favourite gamefish may be different, yet these tips and hints should provide you with additional information that will help you become a more productive fisherman and there "a happy sportfisherman".

General Fishing Tips

* When fishing stained water try changing to a lure with a sound chamber, sometimes a little noise will wake up those lunkers.

* If you are trying to catch a trophy fish, generally speaking, the larger the lure the bigger the odds of hooking a large fish. Some fish such as musky and pike have been known to attack fish their own size.

* Never leave rubber or vinyl baits such as rubber worms, grubs or skirts exposed to other plastics in a tackle box that is not "worm proof". The different chemicals may react and damage one another.

* Make a comparative price list of tackle items you normally buy, such as reels, rods and tackle. By referring to your list before you buy, you can be aware of which outlet has the lowest price in town.

* Never change the size of the trebles on an artificial lure unless you're willing to do some fine tuning. Most artificial lures have been designed to work properly with certain size and weight of hooks.

* Remember to rinse out your net after every catch. Your net will not only smell cleaner, but will last longer.

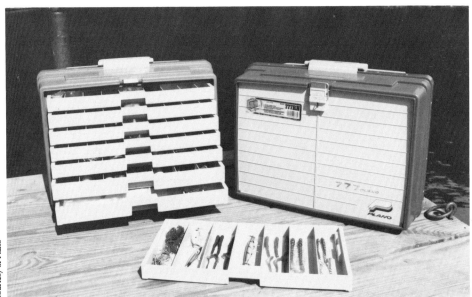

courtesy of Plano

* If you are just starting into the sport of fishing, don't buy too much equipment and tackle. Start out with a small assortment of lures that will catch fish in your area; to find what these are, check with a local fishing club member or other knowledgeable friends.

* When you are using a float with bait ideally you should weigh the line below the float with sinkers enough just to keep the float up. This way you will see the slightest tap and the fish will feel the least resistance when the float starts to go below the surface.

❧ Ninety percent of the tackle on the market is designed to catch the fisherman rather than the fish. Shop for tackle with an objective in mind. Fishing takes patience, and so does lure selection. Don't buy every lure you see, select lures on their own merits, not by the design of the packages.

❧ When using wobbling lures always use a snap or a loose knot which allows the lure action to operate freely. If a wobbling lure is not working properly or is riding on it's side it may be that the knot is restricting the action of the lure.

❧ If you get a hole or rip in your waders or hip boots, silicone in a tube is an excellent product to seal and patch these areas. Make sure the rubber is dry, sand lightly to form a rough surface, then smear the silicone on the inside and outside of the damaged area, let dry before using.

❧ If the top of your rod always gets loose and shifts, try adding some wax to the male furrule. It will stop it from slipping and it will be easy to take apart.

❧ When taking your rod apart never hold on to the guides and try to yank it apart. Always hold the main blank as close to the furrule as possible and use a twisting motion to separate the pieces.

❧ When you have ended your fishing and are travelling home, clean any fish that you will be keeping and store them in a cool place in your vehicle. If you do not have a cooler use newspaper and large ferns or leaves to insulate your fish in the trunk of your car. Don't leave fish whole and in a closed plastic bag, this will raise the inside temperature even more and the liquid in the digestive tract of the fish may taint its meat.

❧ For a lanyard to hold your sunglasses around your neck or line clippers that won't rot or break, get about 18 inches of heavy monofilament line in about 40 to 60 lb. test, form a loop at each end (with the line clippers passing through one of the loops), and secure the loops with clip-on electrical splices. For your sunglasses, tie the monofilament line around the arm and seal the knot by melting some of the line.

General Fishing Tips

♣ When you are putting fish on a stringer never put the fish on a stringer through it's gills, always use the lower part of the jaws. This area is much stronger and will ensure that your fish will not rip off you stringer.

♣ Don't let your fishing trip be ruined by a broken spring in your casting reel. Save the little springs in your worn-out ball point pens. Carry several in your tacklebox. They can be easily modified to fit and work in your reel.

♣ Most boat fishermen carry a small tool kit in their boat, but how many toss in a tube of Super Glue, a couple of extra rod tips, some line wrap and maybe some clear nail polish or winding finish? There's nothing worse than losing the tip off your favorite rod. Be ready to make these "on the water" repairs to save some valuable fishing time.

♣ Fish parallel to weed lines for more productivity. Also cast to and into open pockets for more fish.

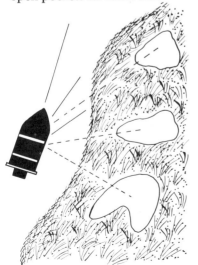

♣ After removing the hook from your catch, leave the fish in the net. Weigh the fish and net. Release your catch and now weigh the net. Subtract the net's weight from your reading and you'll have your fish's weight without harming its return to the water.

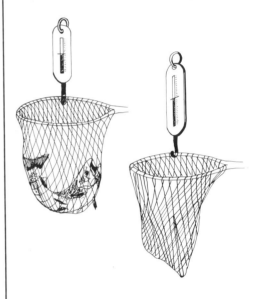

♣ A sharp hook when placed by its point on the nail of your finger should not slip off.

♣ If no steel leaders are available connect several snap-swivels together, they will form a temporary leader.

♣ If your reel starts to slip in the reel seat, use some electrical tape to anchor the reel more permanently. You can tighten it as much as you want, it will keep your hands off the metal and you can remove it whenever you want.

❧ Anglers sometimes go overboard when it comes to buying tackle. It's more important to have a wide range of colours in your tackle box. Stay with the better-known lures. All you have to do is use colour-prism tape to make your colour change.

❧ Drifting is a favorite technique used by many fishermen, for many species of fish. If your boat is drifting over weed beds and shoals too fast, tie a plastic pail to a strong line attached to your boat. The drag can be adjusted by the amount of rope you let out.

❧ Where there is choppy water, it's best to fish the windy shore. Your body will be partially concealed because the water actually distorts the fish's vision.

❧ The less you handle a fish, the better chance it has to survive. Try to keep the fish in water, unhooking the lure with the use of long needlenose pliers. If the fish is completely exhausted, support the belly of the fish while holding its tail. Remember, don't move the fish from head to tail in the water (back and forth). You will force too much water through its gills and it may possibly die a short time later.

❧ Store-bought hooks are usually quite dull. All hooks should be sharpened before use. The larger the hooks the blunter they will usually be. There are several electrical battery operated hook sharpeners on the market. They are compact, powerful and will last most of the fishing season on a couple of "C" size batteries.

General Fishing Tips

🍁 Polarized sunglasses are a must when fishing, but remember: yellow or amber lenses are great for cloudy or dull days, dark lenses should be worn on sunny days and when ice fishing. Remember reflection from the snow can really tire you out. The advantage in the summer months is that you'll see the fish before they see you.

🍁 Think like a fish and you may catch more of them. Fishing is best under these conditions when the day is slightly overcast; or in the morning, late evening, when the water is slightly discoloured and in heavy cover areas.

🍁 Pattern fishing consists of certain combinations of circumstances when conditions like water temperature, clarity, structure are the same throughout the lake. No matter where you go, the pattern should work and you should catch fish.

🍁 Over a period of time your luncheon cooler and/or thermos can obtain a musty smell. This can be solved by putting in a couple of tablespoons of common baking soda on top of the water. Just shake the solution up and rinse a few times with clean water.

🍁 One of the most important tips in angling for most species is to check the contents of the stomach. You may only bring in one or two fish a morning, but if for example a largemouth had a couple of crayfish in its cavity, you should decide to use live crayfish or crayfish colour lures in the afternoon. The size, shape and colour of their feed are all important factors that may help you bag more fish.

🍁 When fishing for pike and musky because of their large teeth, steel leaders or large snap swivels should be used on lures and with live bait.

❧ Many anglers are not aware of the serious side effects due to cold winds. Cold-blowing winds or moving fast in a boat during cold weather can be harmful to the body. Pay close attention to this wind chill table and dress accordingly.

❧ When you are fishing stained water or if you are trying to make fish strike, fluorescent colour lures will work better than natural colour lure. Natural colours fade in deeper or stained water, whereas, fluorescent colours retain their colours.

WIND CHILL TABLE

W I N D   M.P.H.   **F. Dry-bulb Temperature**

(EQUIVALENT TEMPERATURE) – Equivalent in cooling power on exposed flesh under calm conditions

WIND	35	30	25	20	15	10	5	0	-5	-10	-15	-20	-25	-30	-35	-40	-45
calm	35	30	25	20	15	10	5	0	-5	-10	-15	-20	-25	-30	-35	-40	-45
5	33	27	21	16	12	7	1	-6	-11	-15	-20	-26	-31	-35	-41	-47	-54
10	21	16	9	2	-2	-9	-15	-22	-27	-31	-38	-45	-52	-58	-64	-70	-77
15	16	11	1	-6	-11	-18	-25	-33	-40	-45	-51	-60	-65	-70	-78	-85	-90
20	12	3	-4	-9	-17	-24	-32	-40	-46	-52	-60	-68	-76	-81	-88	-96	-103
25	7	0	-7	-15	-22	-29	-37	-45	-52	-58	-67	-75	-83	-89	-96	-104	-112
30	5	-2	-11	-18	-26	-33	-41	-49	-56	-63	-70	-78	-87	-94	-101	-109	-117
35	3	-4	-13	-20	-27	-35	-43	-52	-60	-67	-72	-83	-90	-98	-105	-113	-123

❧ Most fish prefer a given water temperature during different parts of the year. If you own a temperature probe, you can find the species of fish at the same depth and temperature throughout the lake.

❧ If you are fishing shallow water with many snags and are using artificial lures, changing the lower (front) treble to a large single hook will decrease your odds of getting hung-up on bottom and will still hook fish extremely well.

❧ Night fishing is best with fluorescent line and a small black light. A second choice would be a flashlight or type of light rigged to the forehead (e.g. miner's hat).

❧ When fishing murky water, it's best to use fluorescent coloured lures and/or ones that have rattles or internal beads.

❧ No matter what the season, an extra pair of socks for a midday change will make your fishing trip a more enjoyable one. Just think how fresh your feet will feel.

General Fishing Tips

* Practice these 5 tips for better casting.

  1. Thinner line will cast better.

  2. Don't overfill your reel.

  3. Line up and keep your eye continually on the target area.
  4. Watch your backswing and follow through. Don't go back further than 10 o'clock.
  5. Casting is all in the wrist, control your cast, don't muscle it.

* Every Province has their own fishing regulations, sport fishing licences, enforcement laws, and catch and size limits. Take heed, and be a true sportfisherman with "pride".

* Fishing maps of over 500 lakes in Ontario alone can be purchased from the District Office or, the Public Service Centre, Ministry of Natural Resources, Whitney Block, Queen's Park, Toronto, Ont. M7A 1W3. Or the Canada Map Office, 615 Booth St. Ottawa, Ontario K1A OE9.

* If you land a Ministry tagged fish, forward the tag to the nearest District Office of the Ministry of Natural Resources, along with the following information: your name, address, the species of fish, its length and weight, where it was caught, the date and whether the fish had more than one tag. If possible, Ministry officials would like you to send a sample of six to eight scales.

* The best winter wear for warmth contains "goose down". If you want to stay warm while fishing throughout the winter months, buy this type of insulating material in your clothing.

* "Short staking" is also an excellent technique to keep the fish from getting its head down and diving. Just use some short lifting strokes as well as some quick pumping action on your rod and your landing percentage should improve.

20

❧ Whether you fish the Great Lakes or the smaller inland water, you should be aware of how to forecast weather. By studying cloud formations, you'll be able to decide with fair accuracy what the weather will be like throughout that day and the next.

❧ If you're fishing in strong winds or cold rain, apply a thin base of Vaseline to your face. It'll held prevent chapping, and cracked lips.

❧ Safety and first-aid should always go hand-in-hand when you're fishing. Every first-aid kit should include: bandaids of different sizes, a gauze bandage, an elastic one, tape, tweezers, aspirin and sunscreen lotion.

❧ You never know when matches will come in handy. To insure that they'll always work; keep them dry, use the wooden kind and waterproof them by coating the heads with nail polish.

❧ When using snap-swivels and leaders for fish such as pike and muskie always use black over silver. Black is almost invisible even in the clearest water, whereas silver is extremely noticable.

❧ A plastic jug frozen with water keeps many things cold and as it melts, it can provide you with a thirst-quenching drink. For a change though, try freezing lemonade, fruit juice or even a soft drink.

❀ Pick a fishing spot with plenty of casting room and away from the crowds especially if you are fishing from the bank. In a lake avoid areas that have too many hang-ups on the bottom.

❀ Choose lures that won't be lost easily, for example; spinnerbait for bass, weedless lures for most fish in shallower weedy water.

❀ Take some snacks with you and make sure to have many breaks if the fishing is slow and enjoy the scenery around you.

❀ Don't over-coach. The first time fisherman will do better if you let them make some mistakes, then point out how they can be corrected.

❀ Stress catch and release, but remember that a first-timer will be especially proud of his or her catch. Let them take pride and show it off.

❀ Don't get up too early or stay out too late. It's better to leave the person wanting more than taking him home too tired.

❀ Don't release live bait-fish into waters other than those from which they were originally taken. Illegal release can seriously damage some fisheries.

❀ Don't take your best equipment, just so YOU don't start fishing too seriously and forget about your friend and so that if anything does get broken it won't mean a friendship.

Tackle Care

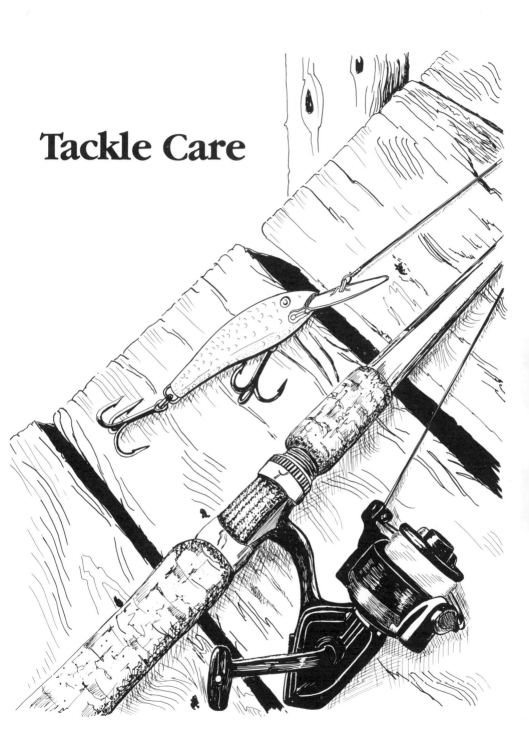

Tackle Care

Don't be fooled into buying tackle just to get by. Learn to match the right reel to rod, rod to line and line to lure and not only will you become more proficient in catching fish but you'll probably land the bigger ones that usually slip away. For example, knots need to be tied properly, equipment used accordingly and protected to insure a long life.

With the price of tackle these days, storage and care have become very important to even the occassional fisherman. Far too many anglers have the unfortunate experience of poorly caring for their tackle, going on a fishing trip, only to find their lures and plugs in very poor condition. Once you've got your tackle set, proper care will be of utmost importance. No single chapter can possibly deal with all the tips and hints available to care and protect ones' fishing gear. Certain ideas and guidelines will indeed save the angler time, money and most of all headaches.

Since tackle care involves such a large grouping, we have sub-divided this chapter into line, lures, rod, reel and miscellaneous to make it easier to review the tips and hits.

Line

* When purchasing fishing line check for date of manufacturing or ask store attendant if the line has been stocked recently. Always purchase the freshest line possible.

* When loading a spool with fresh line it's important to fill your reel properly, to prevent line twists, for spinning reels always fill the reel directly from the spool which should be held with a pencil. For baitcasting reels the spool should be held in the same manner. It is important that you do not set tension on the incoming line with your fingers, this may cause line twist. Always set the tension on the line being spooled by having the person holding the pencil and new spool put pressure on the sides of the spool.

* Whenever you want to move sinkers up or down the line whether it's split shot, twist sinkers or bell sinkers, the sinkers should be removed from the line and then re-attached to the desired position rather than sliding the sinkers up and down and weakening the line.

* Flourescent line has its moments like late evening, night fishing, even fishing murky waters but just remember if you see it, so can the fish. These high visibility lines do in fact spook fish.

* Whenever you are using light line less than 6 lb. test, you should take extreme care when adding any terminal tackle to the line. Floats should be held to the line with rubber tubing rather than wire springs or tying.

* If you have trouble poking your line through an eye of a hook, get a needle threader for about 25 cents at a store that sells sewing supplies. It does a quick and easy job.

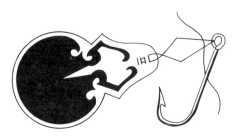

* Doubling the line to tie the knot doesn't necessarily make the knot stronger, this can actually weaken the knot. It's much better to tie one of the better knots on the single line.

* If your fishing line appears chalky and you see a powdery residue coming off the line it means it is starting to deteriorate and it should be replaced.

* At times it is very difficult to pick out frayed areas on your line by simply passing the line through your hand. If you pass the line through your lips you will feel the slightest wear spots on the line.

* Another tip on saving line is to empty your spool when the line gets worn and reel it on the opposite way, this will let you use that portion of your line that was previously buried and unused.

* When trimming a knot always leave ⅛" of lead so that if the knot starts to slip a little, it won't come undone.

❧ Be careful with sections of unwanted monofilament. Birds, animals even your motor will suffer eventually. The best place to dispose of it is in the rubbish. If you're on a long backpacking trip, melt it in the fire.

❧ Always store fishing line in a dark, cool, dry place away from chemicals and other toxic substances. Many people store their fishing rods and reels along with their outboard motor and gas tank in a garage or storage shed. The best place to store your line is in a closet.

❧ Many people will add lubricants to their monofilament line to make it pass over their guides more smoothly or will add other chemicals to keep their guides from freezing in cold weather. Make sure that what you are using won't damage your fishing line, and also be aware that those foreign scents on your line can turn fish off.

❧ When trying a knot moisten the line before cinching it up leaving an ⅛ of an inch after the knot for slippage.

❧ To prevent a line break when fighting a fish, make sure that your drag is not set too tight on the reel. A good rule of thumb is to set the drag at no more than half the pound/test of the line. Make sure you test your line all the way through your rod guides and not a few inches from your reel face. Tie the line to a stationary object, put a bend in the rod and apply full drag. Now loosen the drag until you can back away easily with the rod tip bent.

❧ An easy way to check and see if your fishing line is set for battle; tie an overhand knot and determine whether it cuts the line under reasonable pressure. If it does, move up your line and trim off the weak fragments until there's good holding strength.

Line

* Split-shot sinkers should be squeezed tight with your fingers onto the line and not with pliers or teeth to prevent any friction or line damage.

* When fishing very clear water a lighter leader may be used to increase your natural presentation. For example, you may have 8 lb. test line on your reel, by using a swivel you can attach a length of 2 or 4 lb. test line about 2 feet long and then attach your hook and other terminal tackle carefully to the leader.

* Always lubricate your knot with saliva or water as your are tightening it.

* Never tighten a knot with your fingernails, always use the inside of your finger tips to draw the knot tight.

* When fishing is shallow, rocky or stumpy water always check the last 3-5' of line for line nicks or scrapes. At times line can be weakened as much as 90% by being constantly in contact to rough bottom structure in the water.

* The best way to take the twist out of your fishing line is to remove your lure and trail the line behind your boat at a moderate speed. Try to let out as much line as possible, even 200 feet.

* Even top-rated knots fail when tied incorrectly and in a hurry, without proper attention to details. Remember, avoid twisting lines, pull loops slowly, wet your line and pull all knots tight. Most anglers know how to tie at least two fishing knots. Here are a few for you to memorize and master.

Improved Clinch Knot

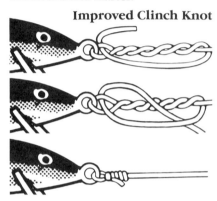

Trilene Knot

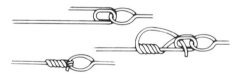

Palomar Knot

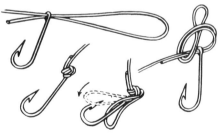

* A knot should be re-tied whenever 6 or more fish are landed, especially fish such as musky and pike with pronounced teeth.

🍁 For people who like to attach their spinning lures directly to their line they can tie a swivel 10 to 14 inches up the line, that way the lure looks as natural as possible and the line won't twist.

🍁 Spoons tend to lose their high-quality lustre over a period of time. Take some water that potatoes were boiled in and place in your tarnished spoons. Leave them overnight and the next day they should shine like new.

🍁 Stryofoam or cork strips attached to your aluminum boat's gunwale can make ideal spots to hang and dry your lures before entering them into your tackle box.

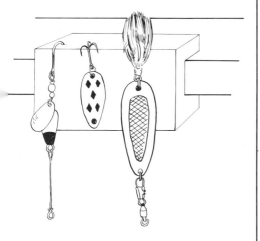

🍁 Pork rind is effective for many species but not cheap. Being reuseable, it's necessary to keep the pork rind from drying out. You can either wrap your pig'n jig in a wet sponge or cloth or you can even store it in a small plastic container. When you're done for the day, just put it back in its original jar.

🍁 Believe it or not, an ordinary pencil eraser will remove shallow rust accumulation on most chrome-plated fishing products.

🍁 Great sales can be found near the end of each fishing season. This is the best time to purchase top-quality fishing tackle.

🍁 With a little hot water and some strong detergent you can restore your plastic skirted baits and worms quite easily. Remember to take the hooks out and just knead a handful of them, rinse and repeat.

🍁 Large lures become difficult to store in an average-sized tackle box. Therefore, here's an inexpensive solution. For $5 or so, you can purchase a styrofoam cooler where you can just push the hooks into the top edges and let the lures lay in the inner walls.

🍁 Keep hooks needle sharp at all times. By using a file, stone or even the new electric sharpener, you'll cut your misses at least by 50%.

🍁 Slight modifications to the eyelet of many lures can decrease or increase the action on the lure. Using small pliers you can fine tune most lures to help entice those lazy fish to bite.

Lures

♣ When using spinning type lures such as spinners, spoons or jigs, always be sure to use a swivel to prevent severe line twisting. Snap swivels should be as small as possible. Swivels with ball bearings are much more efficient than standard swivels. Two high quality swivels are Berkley Lock Snap swivels (ball bearing) and Sampo swivels (ball bearing).

♣ The nice thing about using phosphorescent lures on salmon and many other freshwater gamefish is that you can increase the lures glow by flashing it with a camera flash or powerful flashlight.

♣ Keep several pieces of prism tape in your tackle box. This little addition in supplies will reduce the number of lures you need to carry or for that matter buy. When the fish start hitting a certain colour, just apply the appropriate coloured tape to your lure.

♣ To prevent rust and in turn ruining your lures and baits, run a hot-air hair dryer over them as soon as you get home to get rid of the moisture.

♣ Quality not quantity is the issue when it comes to buying fishing tackle. Buy the best you can afford, mechanics and carpenters do. You'll think more positive when fishing, cast farther, more accurately and probably catch more fish.

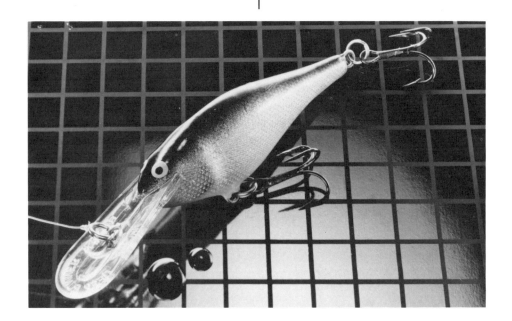

❦ By encircling the top edge of your rod case with your thumb and forefinger, you'll prevent the rod guides and even the windings from catching the hard lip and getting damaged.

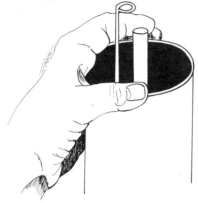

❦ An old bottle of your wife's nail polish can come in handy. By keeping one in your tackle box, you can easily repair loose or frayed rod guide windings.

❦ By revolving your rod slowly while varnishing your rod windings you not only have fewer drips and runs but the over-all job looks very professional.

❦ Two piece rods very often are hard to separate. Therefore, before putting your rod together, rub oil from the skin on your nose over the ferrule. This lubricates the connection so the rod will separate easily when it's time to pack up.

❦ You can often pick up a great deal on rods and reels for the price of repairs alone from sporting stores. Many anglers leave their fishing tackle unclaimed for months and just collect dust.

❦ Many anglers put hundreds of hours fishing in one season and casting fatigue at some point or another will always set it. To help alleviate this problem you can sand down the cork grip to an oval shape with coarse sandpaper then fine. There's nothing like a fitted grip for comfort and ease in casting.

❦ To pick out any damaged areas on your rod guides or reel that may be damaging your line use a cotton swab and go over each guide and tip, pass the swab over your roller on the bail of a spinning reel or the line guide on your baitcaster. The swab will leave traces of cotton wherever, there are burs or worn areas that can damage your line.

❦ Many anglers put hundreds of hours fishing in one season and casting fatigue at some point or another will always set it. To help alleviate this problem you can sand down the cork grib to an oval shape with coarse sandpaper then fine. There's nothing like a fitted grip for comfort and ease in casting.

Sanded Down

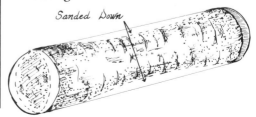

Reels

* Before loading up your reel with new monofilament, soak the spool of line in water for a few hours even overnight. The line memory will relax and it will transfer easier onto your reel.

* The best place to store the new line you bought on sale or your filled reel is in a cool, dark place. Hot sun and tackle boxes are your worst choice.

* Reels with trigger line pick-up are great for casting but for jig fishermen they can be a nuisance. All reels with trigger line pick-up will have a bail that will rotate freely ¼ to ½ of the diameter of the spool at a time. This means that if you are not retrieving the line or casting, but jigging up and down, the bail will rotate and this will result in loose line, also when setting the hook if your hand is not on the handle the line may not go tight instantly when you pull back because the bail will rotate by itself.

* Baitcasting and spinning reels sometimes get tangled beyond recognition. An easy way to clear the line tangles is with a small crochet hook (size 4 or 6). Just store it in your tackle box of goodies.

* A little lubricant on reels is good however, be careful not to apply too much. Dirt, dust even sand can get trapped by the excess oil. Always clean and store your reels properly but oil sparingly.

* If you want your reel to operate efficiently don't overfill your spool; ⅛ of an inch to the lip is just fine. Secondly, make sure you applied some moderate tension when filling your reel.

* If your monofilament line remains on your reel unused for a period of time, it can quite easily snarl, form bird nests and in general give you poor overall casting. A good idea to help eliminate this problem would be to soak the line an hour or so before your next fishing excursion.

* If you drop your reel in dirt or sand make sure to rinse it in water throughly to clean the reel and line. Abrasive material on the line can be ground into guides and reel parts, thus wearing these parts which will result in line damage.

* For the beginner baitcaster a magnetic reel will help you to avoid line twists or "over-runs", but magnetic reels usually have oil-less bearings rather than ball bearings which tend to wear faster under prolonged use.

❧ If you want smoother and longer casts from your spinning reel, just add some car wax on the contact lip of your spool. Make sure you buff the wax completely.

❧ When a baitcaster is being stored, always let-off on the drag completely. Reels which are stored with the drag set tight may end up having a locked drag because of the washer and shim system in the drag.

❧ When casting with a baitcaster, the wrist should be snapping the cast out and not the extended arm. Using the wrist will give you greater casting distance and will be less tiring. A trick that will help you to learn to use your wrist is to place a pocket wallet under your casting arm pit, if you drop your wallet when casting you are casting improperly and using your arm, if the wallet doesn't fall you are casting properly and using your wrist.

❧ For the average freshwater fisherman a high capacity spinning reel will hold much more line than will be used. A way to save on monofilament line is to purchase an arbour to fill the back of the spool or to fill the bottom of the spool with older line just as a filler. The average fisherman never uses more than the first 60 to 80 yards of line.

❧ Spinning reels are much better for line control and casting with lighter line such as 2 to 6 lb. test especially under windy conditions.

❧ If you are an ultralight fisherman you should look for the reel with the smoothest drag. Rear reel mount drags are much easier to work than star drags located on the spools of spinning reels.

❧ For continuous casting and retrieving lures, high gear ratio reels are much better than low gear ratio reels. For example; a 5:1 gear ratio reel will pick up more more line with one rotation of the reel handle than a 3.5:1 gear ratio reel. The gear ratio describes how many times the bail turns in respect to the handle. Therefore, with a 5:1 gear ratio, every time you turn the handle once around, the bail will rotate 5 times.

❧ If you fish with heavier line you will be better off using a baitcasting reel. Baitcasting reels are ideal for trolling because of their higher line capacity and low gear ratio.

❧ When choosing a baitcasting reel always match the reel weight to the rod. When the outfit is held at the reel, it should feel balanced and light.

❧ Baitcasters with "V" spools will increase the length of your casts and will also aid you in decreasing bird nests or backlashes.

Miscellaneous

🍁 Remember to protect your premium monofilament against the sun's untraviolet rays. These damaging rays will not only shorten its useful life but may cause it to break more readily under the strain of a trophy fish.

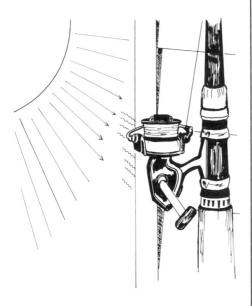

🍁 When fishing big game fish like pike and muskies, your braided-wire leaders occasionally get bent. Stretch the leader tight and rub it back and forth across your knee. The friction heats it up realigning the leader to its original position, straight.

🍁 It's no fun fighting a heavyweight on ultra-light gear or a featherweight on a heavy-action outfit. Match your tackle to your gamefish for maximum fun and enjoyment.

🍁 The best all round knife blade is a stainless one. It takes a little longer to sharpen it but at least it won't rust. Most other blades have carbon steel blades and tend to discolour over a period of time. Whatever your choice keep its sharp blade protected in some kind of sheath.

🍁 There are only a few gamefish in which you might have to use a wire leader. Sure the leader is great when it comes to muskie but with the other fresh water species, the leader just deadens the action of the lure.

🍁 Some tackle boxes crack with rough and hard use. Don't throw it away, just use a plastic pipe joint cement, hold the crack closed while the cement welds and you've got yourself a working tackle box again.

🍁 By cementing a sheet of sandpaper to the bottom of your sharpening stone box you'll eliminate sliding and in turn a possible slip of the blade while sharpening.

Storage

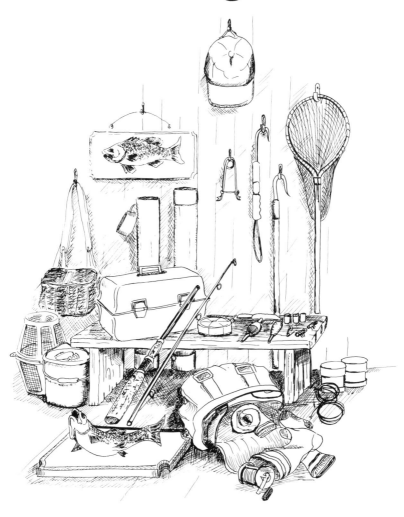

Storage

Whether you're on the road, at home or in your boat, fishing storage requires some forethought and care. Most anglers are so excited about having some particular time to go fishing that they forget about the major problems that occurr when trying to pack their car, boat or knapsack.

It's important for a fisherman to have a good understanding of how to take care of his tackle but its just as important to store his equipment safely for trouble-free use and long life. Whether a fisherman is storing extra line, rods or reels for the season, he should be aware of some important tips that will insure the longevity of his equipment.

Packing and storing fishing equipment for a fly-in or weekend fishing trip is also very important. Many rods and reels are broken and mistreated annually by not having packaged them properly for transit from car to plane; to boat etc.

On another note, when has an angler not left something behind when travelling to his favourite fishing spot? For example, just the use of a simple check list can be an inexpensive insurance against forgetting something on a fishing trip.

Over the years, manufacturers have designed unique storage compartments, satchels and other devices to solve the problem of storage for would-be anglers. However, the cost of these items is another story. By trying some of these helpful tips and hints you should be able to save not only money but also some valuable fishing time by keeping your equipment in top shape.

Storage

- Plastic bags will help encourage corrosion through moisture build-up. A better method for keeping dirt and dust out of your reel machine is to place them in cloth bags. Just wrap them in pieces of cloth using elastic bands to secure them in place.

- Identification tags for your personal fishing equipment can be easily made from expired credit cards. After cutting them down to the size you want just punch or drill holes in the corner of the tags. You can even reinforce the holes with grammets.

- You can easily and quite safely store various sized-hooks and lures in a scrap piece of styrofoam.

- When going on a major fishing trip, pack your reels in socks and place them in a carrying bag or suitcase.

- Here's a tip if you are going on a camping fishing trip. Don't throw away that snarl of fishing line you just cut off your rod. If you lump it in a ball and tie the loose ends around the middle to keep it together, it makes a good scouring pad for the frying pan you just used to cook your fish.

- Every angler carries some sort of knife for multiple uses. A leather sheath will protect the blade and its sharpness however, remember to lightly oil it once in a while. The leather sheath will more than likely hold moisture that could either discolour or rust your blade.

- Garbage bags have multiple uses, one is carrying your foul rain weather gear. The bag will keep your gear dry during your fishing trip but when you return home make sure you air dry your equipment to help prevent mildew and rot.

- Many anglers who like to travel light just use empty Sucrets metal containers to store their ultra light lures and terminal tackle. Wrapping an elastic band will prevent it from opening in your pouch or bag.

- Reels require careful maintenance, not only on a regular basis but on an annual strip down. Keep them away from dirt and grime, after each trip, wash the reel if necessary to remove algae, dirt and dust. On spinning reels remove the spool and wash it separately. Treat the reels with oil or WD-40 to remove moisture and protect moving parts.

You don't need to buy expensive rod cases when going on a distant fishing trip. Purchase lengths of PBS plastic piping in the 4" diameter and cement a bottom cap and tape a top cap on. It will last forever and is less expensive.

Remember to take a camera on every fishing trip, most fishermen don't want the bother but then regret not having captured the fish on film, and when you least expect it you can hook into that trophy fish and later prove you caught it with the photo.

When you are travelling in a boat in between fishing spots and you are using live bait, to keep it moist and on your hook take a film container, make a hole and a slit in the lid and fill partially with water. Slip you bait inside and fit the line through the slit in the lid and seal top. This container will keep your bait moist and supply ready to use when you stop moving.

A zip-locked pencil holder is also a super and inexpensive waterproof case to hold your wallet and valuable papers, licenses etc.

Blocks of ice keep alot longer than cubed ice. So if you're looking at keeping fish on ice for a period of time use block ice. In fact, even ½ blocks can be used if your storage area is tight for room.

An egg carton can become a useful storage compartment box. Whether you're working on some lures, terminal tackle on your reel, the egg carton works out just great for temporary storage and separation of parts.

Store all fishing rods on proper rod racks in your home. Rods should stand upright and shouldn't lean against walls or lay horizontal for long periods of time. Rods will take on a warp if they remain in the same stressed position for months.

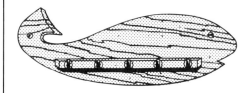

Christmas wrapping tubes are great for storing your topographical maps and charts. Each tube can be marked and labelled for easy access and organization.

If a fisherman uses his reverse reel handle setting when a fish wants to take line, the fisherman can back reel to let out the specific amount of line and then reel forward when the fish tries to pick up line. This provides the light line enthusiast with total line control.

Storage

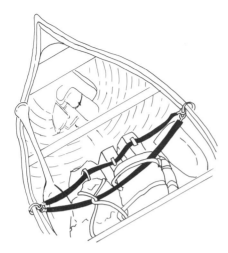

🍁 Elastic motorcycle straps can secure alot of items while fishing. While in a canoe secure all your major items in case of a spill-over. All you have to do is pass the strap through all your gear like your tackle box handles and then attach the ends to your gunwales. You may get wet but at least you won't lose your valuable equipment.

🍁 The best way to protect your topographical charts and maps for life is by a procedure called "thermofaxing". Another less expensive method is to cover the entire surface with transparent contact sheeting which is sold in most hardware departments.

🍁 When you are travelling in a boat in between fishing spots and you are using live bait, to keep it moist and on your hook take a film container, make a hole and a slit in the lid and fill partially with water. Slip your bait inside and fit the line through the slit in the lid and seal top. This container will keep your bait moist and supple, ready to use when you stop moving.

🍁 PVC or ABS plastic tubing, even golf tubes can be set up to store your rods at home or in your boat.

🍁 Remember to loosen the drag all the way when storing your reels over the season. Loosening the tension of the spring on your drag will extend the life of your reel.

🍁 Save those empty margarine containers, they are usually non-breakable, rustproof plastic with leak-proof lids. They make great storage jars for your baits.

🍁 Try using a 4-6" square Tupperware container for carrying an extra roll of graph paper, fuses, matches and other small items in your boat. When the lid is on tight it is completely waterproof.

🍁 **Casting reels** – Oil the handles and any other oil ports on the reel, grease the level wind pawl and gear.

🍁 Many 35mm film manufacturers like FUGI are now making their film cannisters in clear plastic. What a great place to store small tackle items such as your swivels, split-shots and different size hooks.

❦ An easy way to store terminal tackle like swivels and snaps is onto safety pins. Just thread the same size swivels onto a particular safety pin and another size on another.

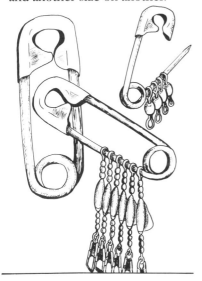

❦ When travelling, just lay your rods tip-to-butt before storing them in a golf-tube type container. You'll have less worries about breakage. For more protection you can even place a wooden dowel into the tube for added strength.

❦ **Spincast reels** - Oil the handle, thumb release and the pick-up pin inside the cap.

❦ **Spinning Reels** - Oil the bushing under the roller, the reel handle, and use a few drops at the points where the bail attaches to the rotating cup.

❦ **Fly reels** - Oil the handle, the spool and the click mechanism on the inside. Taking time to do these simple maintanance steps will give you smoother performance, longer life, and easier fishing.

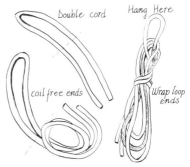

❦ Ropes are used at one point or another by fishermen and boaters alike. An easy method to bundle a rope is to first fold the cord in half. Coil the doubled cord beginning with the free ends and then wrap the loop end around the bundle one or more times. The last step before hanging or other storage is to thread it through the upper end.

Fishing for Largemouth Bass

Largemouth Bass

Fishing for Largemouth Bass

COMMON NAMES: black bass, bigmouth, largemouth

When someone says bass, the first things that come to mind are probably lily pads, reeds, fallen trees, stumps - all of which usually equal "largemouth". The angler also can see images of a "big mouth" coming to the surface to inhale a surface lure. By the way, this is one of the most popular methods for catching largemouth bass.

When water temperatures reach 62 to 68 degrees F, the largemouth will start to spawn. Soon after it will move to warm water bays, making him the most sought after shallow water gamefish. A slight change in temperature can determine whether the fish will feed agressively or lie neutral, secluded in cover or in a heavy weedline.

Largemouth in Ontario average 2 to 4 pounds and trophy fish in the 5 to 8 pound class are boated every year. There are many ways to catch largemouth using artifical lures. Yet, live bait fishing is also a successful technique since worms, frogs, and crayfish are part of their diet. These tips will insure more "bassin-fun" on your next trip.

Fishing for Largemouth Bass

✤ The nice thing about spinnerbaiting for bass; you can interchange skirts, blades and trailers for different occasions limiting your purchasing cost. However, you should have at least one long arm and one short-arm model so that you can fish both deep and shallow, weedy or open water.

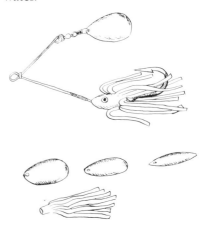

✤ Bass must make do with the structure or cover that's made available to them. By searching for these unsuspected areas big bass may become a reality.

✤ On many southern lakes wind and carp will up-root vegetation that will be blown to one area of a lake. This floating vegetation can be called "slop". "Slop" provides ideal surface cover for largemouths. Try fishing these areas at different times of the day.

✤ On many southern lakes surrounded by summer resorts, human traffic in the form of water skiing, pleasure boating and swimming force many largemouths to adapt to nightime feeding.

✤ Use fast running surface lures to locate active largemouths in shallow water.

FLOYD'S BUZZER™ (RUBBER SKIRT)

❦ When choosing the right spinnerbait for the right conditions consider these points;

1) Short-arm spinnerbaits are designed for open water, they are not very weedless.

2)Long-arm spinnerbaits are designed for weedy water, they are almost weedless.

3) Single-bladed spinnerbaits will have to be retrieved faster to keep the blades working. These are ideal when bass are very active.

4) Double-bladed spinnerbaits can be fished much slower and will run much shallower and are ideal when fish are less agressive.

❦ When fishing surface lures for bass, always hesitate for a few seconds before setting the hook. Most beginners tend to miss a fish because they set the hook immediately.

❦ The most productive cattails, reeds and lily pads will be those that are close to a drop-off or slightly deeper water. This change may be only 1-3', but these areas can be number one largemouth bass area.

❦ Another way to fish a rubber frog is to cast it on top of pads near an edge of opening, drag and hop the frog over the top of the vegetation. This will get a lot of attention right up until you reach the opening, where you should let the frog rest and wait for an explosive strike.

❦ Surface fishing for bass at night isn't the only technique that works. Use spinner baits, rubber worms and live bait in the same areas that you fish noisy surface lures.

❦ The best time to begin nightfishing is an hour or two before sunset. Get to know the area you will be fishing before the lights go out.

❦ Big bass like protective cover. It's therefore very important to fish dock, trees, stumps and other objects that cast shadows over the water. Check out the sun throughout the day and fish the shady area whenever possible.

Fishing for Largemouth Bass

♣ Full moonlight is easy to night fish in however, no moon at all provides the best overall largemouth bass fishing. Try using noisy popper and black surface lures because their silouette will stand out more than any other colour.

♣ By just adding a split-shot to your spinnerbaits wire shaft, you can make it run deeper.

♣ Whenever fishing "slop", approach carefully and quietly. Drop your bait or lure in every opening that you go by. The largemouths in this type of cover are usually very aggressive and will hit immediately.

♣ The best artificials for fishing the slop are, Johnston's silver minnow, rubber worms and jigs.

♣ Rubber frogs are killers for largemouths in thick weeds. Bill Plumber's Super Frog, Garcia's frog and Mister Twister's Hawg frog are some of the most productive. Fish these as slow as possible right over thick cover.

♣ Many tournament fishermen have won tournaments fishing docks and boathouses. Try casting jigs along side these structures using dark coloured jigs, grubs and worms.

Fishing for Largemouth Bass

* On large rivers such as the St. Lawrence River, look for largemouths in protected bays and smaller streams and creeks that lack current.

* Shallow water largemouths will get turned off with strong winds. If the winds are strong enough, they will leave these shallow water areas and go to the closest deep water.

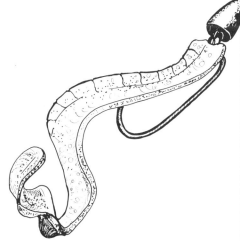

* If you remove a largemouth from a particular spot, go back and try it again, even a few days later. Sooner or later another big one will probably move in. No matter what the area is like, as long as it provides cover, lots of food - other fish will move in.

* One of the best bass lures is the "rubber worm", hook Texas Style. Purple and black are the best colours under most conditions.

* Largemouth bass are most active in water 68 to 78 degrees Fahrenheit. Even then many will be in protected shallow water areas.

"Johnson's Silver Minnow"

* Variation is the spice of life. When the largemouth refuse to hit your plug on a slow retrieve, try the opposite. Retrieve your lure as soon as it hits the water, try to stir up alot of noise and those lazy bass should eventually strike your specific presentation.

* Largemouth bass often go for surface lures throughout the day. A weedless lure like the "Johnson's Silver Minnow" with a strip of pork rind worked atop of lily pads usually triggers the big bass to hit.

Fishing for Largemouth Bass

* If you are fishing the edges of weedy areas using live bait or artificial lures and you can't get any fish, try using a weedless lure and cast right across the middle of the thick weeds. At times largemouths will sit in the thickest cover.

* One way to correct short hits by bass, big or small is to add a "stinger" hook in a regular or weedless style.

* Any bass fishermen will agree that topwater lure fishing is one of the most exciting there is. By using noisy surface plugs such as the well-known jitterbug or buzzbait, largemouth can be drawn out of the tightest cover. Make sure to pause at least 2 seconds before setting the hook. The best times to use this technique are early morning or late evening, preferably over calm waters.

* When bass are finicky about their food, try using a plastic worm fished across points, near wood, trees and other thick cover. Bass can pick up the movement of these slinky baits even in the darkest night.

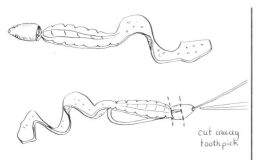

cut away
toothpick

❧ When using a texas-rigged plastic worm, wedge the worm-sinker by inserting a piece of toothpick in the hole after the line has been fed through it. This will keep your sinker close to the worm at all times allowing a better drop and a more natural presentation.

❧ In many weedbed areas, largemouth are buried deep within the weeds and a conventional size spinner blade will not produce enough vibration to draw these big bruisers out of cover. This is the time to change to a bigger willow-leaf type blade on your spinnerbait.

❧ Bass often hear their prey before they see it. The lateral line serves as a sonar and it is effective up to distances of 20-30'. In deeper or murky water rattling crank baits and spinnerbaits will work well.

❧ When fishing large weedy areas for bass, look for key ambush points that largemouths will use when feeding;

1) Open pockets in a blanket of lily pads.
2) Long finger-like points of either lily pads or thick "slop".
3) Channels or cuts between floating mats of weeds.
4) Weedy points off of straight weedy shorelines.

❧ You can make a strong light-weight push pole for boating in shallow waters from 1 and ¼ inch PVC pipe. Remember to close the pipe with caps at both ends, let dry and you end up with a push pole for less than $10.

Fishing for Largemouth Bass

🍁 Noisy surface plugs like the jitterbug or buzzbait in some cases don't produce. Remember to fish the logjams, docks and other areas of thick cover.

🍁 Even though fishing is usually not too productive during heavy pressure changes, big bass can always be had in tight cover, especially under heavy reed mats and undercut banks.

🍁 Largemouths unlike smallmouths don't like moving water. They will prefer back bays and channels that are quiet.

🍁 Shorter casts will allow better line control and therefore better hook sets.

❧ Help enhance the flavour of your pork rinds by soaking the pieces in solutions of anise oil or fish scents like Dr. Juice.

❧ When fishing for largemouths there are really two ways to get a fish to hit;

Natural presentation - Tempting the fish to take live bait or duplicate live bait with artificials.

Striking presentation - Triggering a strike from instincts by the action of a particular lure you are using.

❧ The best natural presentation for largemouth bass is using frogs, worms, leeches and minnows.

❧ Largemouths love weeds and cover. If you're fishing unfamiliar lakes, look for weeds and you'll find largemouths.

❧ If you plan to seriously fish largemouth bass, consider purchasing a medium action baitcasting outfit. Baitcasters are usually stiffer and can horse bass out of the heaviest cover. Baitcasting reels will hold plenty of heavier line and you will be able to make much more accurate casts.

❧ Thunder storms with lots of lightning can spook bass severely. When fishing after an electrical storm, use lighter lines, smaller lures and make your casts way past the target areas. This will keep the bass from spooking.

❧ Beaver dams are not only appealing to the eye but are also good areas for largemouth. Even after the beavers have moved to other areas the remaining dam structures attract fish year after year.

Fishing for Largemouth Bass

🍁 Largemouth bass are most active before, or during a low pressure system (rainy weather).

🍁 On windy days, always fish the calm sides of points, weed beds and islands for largemouth bass.

🍁 When navigating in shallow water it's important to move through the area as quietly as possible. If you make noise, the fish won't move far, but you can spook them out of casting range or drive them into thick cover where you won't be able to get to them.

🍁 Largemouths love to feed on frogs. Leopard frogs are the most productive. In shallow water fish the frogs on the surface. In deeper water go to a sliding live bait rig.

🍁 Largemouth will be attracted to many types of vegetation that stick out of the water. Look for reeds, cattails, sawgrass, wild rice and bullrush. All these are ideal areas to catch largemouths.

* Old boat houses are prime "lunker" areas. Try casting your lure right inside and be ready.

* Cast parallel to shorelines with heavy cover, secluded backwater areas can hold many bass in a short distance.

* After a thunderstorm fish driftwood or log jams packed at the back of some bays, these areas can hold schools of bass.

* Striking lures for largemouths include flashy crankbaits, spinner baits and surface lures.

* If by chance one of your favourite rubber worms gets ripped, just fuse the damaged part with a match flame. Give it a few minutes to cool before using it on another largemouth.

* In lakes that contain both largemouths and northern pike, the largemouths will usually be forced to live closer to the shorelines. The deeper weed lines will hold mainly pike.

* "Pattern-fishing" for largemouths can be very successful. If you are catching bass in a certain area or type of weed, look for similar areas in different parts of a lake. They should all hold some bass. That's pattern fishing.

* Bass associate with different coloured water, for example, if you are fishing a clear lake for largemouths, look for muddy creeks or areas that have an algae bloom. Bass may concentrate in these "stained water" areas.

* Sometimes you just need that little extra to trigger those largemouth to hit. Try using some pork rind as a trailer for your spinnerbait, even a different coloured twister.

Fishing for Largemouth Bass

❧ Fishing boat channels in front of cottages or around marinas can be very productive. Use rubber worms and work them slow, close to the edge of the shoreline.

❧ In lakes that lack vegetation, look for largemouth bass along the shorelines or in slightly deeper water structure such as rock piles and shoals.

❧ If your favourite bassin shorelines are without fish, move out to the deeper adjacent waters near weed lines. These are always productive, come rain or shine.

❧ Natural baits are always productive. How can a largemouth refuse a helpless frog, minnow or leach. Use a light split shot so the bait can move freely looking as natural as possible.

❧ Bass can see colour and can stand strong sunlight in shallow water. Fish for them right through the day with natural and bright coloured lures.

❧ When fishing lures close to the surface and fish are seen following and not striking, let the lure drop. Most fish can't resist a falling bait.

❧ Spinnerbaits are the easiest lures to use for largemouths. They are quite weedless and can be used along the surface or at deeper depths. They are productive all season long.

Fishing for Smallmouth Bass

Smallmouth Bass

Fishing for Smallmouth Bass

COMMON NAMES: green bass, bronzeback, smalljaws, smallies, smallmouth

The smallmouth bass is glorified as the wildest, strongest fighting fish in warm water. No fish can match the aerial acrobatic display that a smallmouth performs when it's fighting. It's common to see a fighting smallmouth somersaulting into the air with the fish going one way and the lure the other way.

The smallmouth bass is a close cousin of the largemouth, yet the species differ in many ways. Appropriately called the "bronzeback", the smallmouth bass has a copper, dark brown or olive-green side with vertical bars.

Smallmouth bass prefer cooler, clearer water with lots of rocks, drop-offs and shoals. They can be found in most lakes that are between 50 to 80 degrees F in temperature. They will reach weights in excess of 10 pounds, but 1 to 3 pound fish are the most common. Smallmouths do not reach the size of largemouth bass so if you land yourself a 5 pound plus bronzeback – you've automatically nailed yourself a wall-hanger.

Most fishing methods will work for these fish, but generally speaking they will be caught slightly deeper. Being a fairly agressive fish, smallmouths will strike most deep diving plugs such as crankbaits which are very popular for deeper water smallmouths.

Once you locate smallmouths, they are easy and fun to catch. Try fishing deep holes and fast water in rivers and streams. Remember, crayfish are a smallmouth's favourite food. In the summer, smallmouths will roam shorelines and other structures in search of food. Livebait on bottom, surface lures and even flies can be used to catch these spunky fish. One thing for sure, pound for pound, the "bronzeback" will give you all the fight you're looking for. Tasty mealfare too!

Fishing for Smallmouth Bass

🍁 Smallies in southern lakes like weeds close to rough, rocky bottom. To find these productive weed lines, follow any rock pile or bar that leaves a shoreline or island. The weed beds at the end of the rocks could end up to be "honey-holes".

🍁 The best way to tell the difference between smallmouth bass and largemouth bass is to look at the dorsal fins. The largemouth's dorsal fin is connected, whereas, the smallmouth's front dorsal is separate from the rear one.

🍁 In many of our northern lakes there is only scattered vegetation. Trolling the shorelines with small repalas is probably the most effective method to locate smallies. Pick an irregular shoreline and troll in about 10-15′ of water. When you hook a fish, go back and see if there is something special about the spot and try casting.

🍁 Smallmouth are schooling fish. It's common to stumble on a school and catch a limit very quickly.

🍁 By locating structure in deep water you can find schools of smallmouths that are just waiting to be fed. Once you locate some structure try vertical jigging with spoons or jigs, you may hook one fish after another.

🍁 Smallmouths enjoy feeding on crustaceans, therefore smaller baits usually works best, especially jigs.

🍁 Anchoring and still fishing for smallmouth is also very productive. Choose a structure such as gravel, rock or sand bar in 10-20′ of water.

🍁 When fishing smallmouth, be sure not to overlook man-made structure such as old bridge pilings, culverts, bridge abutments, sunken boats or even boat docks. If it look as if it could hold a fish or two it probably will.

🍁 Many people think that smallmouths will only venture into shallow water during spawning, fall feeding sprees, or at night. This is not always true, you'll be amazed how shallow you'll find some smallmouths.

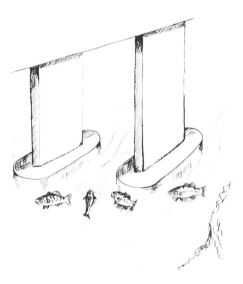

🍁 Bridge pilings and abutments are rarely fished. Try casting crankbaits and jigs for some beauty smallmouths. It never fails there's always smallmouth in these type of areas throughout the season.

Fishing for Smallmouth Bass

♣ Crankbaits are very effective when river fishing. Their fast presentation lets you cover a lot of water quickly. Cranking is also a big fish method, often producing larger fish when live bait and jigs will catch only smaller fish.

RAPALA FAT RAP
(DEEP RUNNING)

♣ **Early summer** Use natural running balsa wood crankbaits with no sound chamber. Shad Raps, Rebel fast trac series and Rapalas Fat raps are good choices fish these slow and retrieve constantly.

Mid-summer Use a variety of crankbaits, go to larger sizes, bright colours and sound chambers.

Fall As the water temperature gets colder go to natural running baits again in naturalized finished. Vary the retrieve when cranking.

♣ River fishing for smallmouth below dams can be very rewarding. Smallmouth will use currents to their advantage. They will find ambush points and they will let their prey come downstream right to them. Any lure or bait approaching them from behind rarely gets a fish's attention. Therefore, fish downstream, it will be more productive than trolling upstream.

♣ Even in the summer months, smallmouths can be located in the shallow rocky shoals in the early morning and late evening hours.

♣ When working shallow waters with jigs, rubber or hair, try dragging the jig bouncing bottom, lift your rod tip and repeat. A different presentation just may help you to box a few for the frying pan.

* When fishing with jigs use the lightest line possible. Most of the action comes from your rod tip movement therefore you jig will drop more natural and have more fancy action using light line.

* Many people don't realize how much fun it is to catch smallmouth bass at night. Heddon Tiny Torpedo, Hulla poppers, dying flutters and small fly poppers are good producers.

* Smallmouth will move into shallow water at night, near structure and also over fairly flat sandy bottoms. Beach areas that are void of fish in the daytime can come alive after dark.

* Trolling at night with shallow running rapalas and surface lures work great for smallmouth bass.

* Never overlook one or two large bolders in the water, smallmouths love to sit in the shade of cracks and rocks. At times these spots produce lunkers.

* By reeling in a crankbait along the rocky shoals, having it actually bounce and touch bottom will often trigger an onlooking smallmouth to hit. The noisy stirred-up bottom usually does the trick.

* Some people also believe that bright sunny days mean poor fishing. Smallmouths will sun themselves in water less than a foot in depth. Under these conditions use a small floating rapala or other minnow type lure that will not dive deep.

* During the summer months smallmouth will be attracted to long points protruding far from shore. In the fall smallmouth will move to short, rounded points near the shoreline that have a good rock structure, or a combination of rocks and weeds.

* Another hot spot for smallmouth is rock piles and slides that have tumbled into the water on a normally regular shoreline. These areas will harbour crayfish and baitfish that will draw smallies.

Fishing for Smallmouth Bass

* Deep diving wobbling lures are one of the top producers for smallmouth bass all season long. Choosing the right "Crank-bait" for different conditions is very important.

* How to locate smallmouths seasonally;

   Early season - Fish will often be in deep water which is close to shore and adjacent to spawning grounds.

   Summer - Smallies will be found all over the lake in deep and shallow water along weed edges and shorelines.

   Fall - Smallmouths will move to deeper water structure from 10-30′ in depth, closest to the main lake basin.

* Smallmouth bass are very territorial, a family or group of bass will occupy a certain area year after year.

* Over 50% of a smallmouth's diet is crayfish. Softshelled crayfish are its favourite.

* On many of our lakes the best way to catch smallmouths is by using minnows, frogs, crayfish, leeches and worms. Still fish or drift shorelines, deep and shallow water structure as well as weed beds and weed lines.

* Look for smallmouth near rocky shoals, drop-offs and stoney points. They may be found where the rocky bottom meets the lake weed lines as well.

ROCKY BOTTOM SIGNALS

Fishing for Smallmouth Bass

❦ There's no question that crayfish are one of the best baits for these fish. Unfortunately, most fishermen hook them through the tail which usually results in missed strikes. The angler should use a long-shanked hook and fasten it to the crayfish with a rubber band and the hook's point near the crayfish's head. Your bait will remain more active and your hook sets will be more productive.

❦ "River-slipping" is an excellent boat control technique that produces smallies. You can jig, cast plugs or troll live bait very effectively. Just face your bow into the current and keep your motor running in gear. The trick is to adjust your throttle so that you are drifting downstream a little slower than the surface current.

❦ Many fishermen become perfectionists when it comes to lure action. Pro or not, if your bassin lure doesn't operate the way you think it should, do some fine tuning yourself. Try bending the tie-on-eye a little at a time until your fine-tuning catches some fish.

❦ One of the best combinations to drift fish for smallies is to use small worm harnesses and worms. Bob-it, Williams fir fly spinners and Hildenbrant spinners all work well.

❦ Look for steep rocky banks with one of more fallen trees in the water. These areas will hold small schools of smallies all season long.

❦ Windy weather usually turns smallmouths on. Fish the shallow sides of shoals, dropoffs and other structure. Smallmouth bass will be drawn to these turbulent water areas to feed on baitfish, crustaceans and aquatic insects.

❦ You can make any crankbait run deeper by adding a worm-weight or splitshot to the line just ahead of the lure.

Fishing for Smallmouth Bass

🍁 Smallmouths can easily be caught fly fishing. Use streamers, wet flies and surface poppers. There is nothing more exciting than setting the hook into a smallmouth that has broken water to take a surface fly.

🍁 Trophy smallmouths can be had in early summer when they are spawning. Just cast jigs or crankbaits near their spawning bed, slide set the hook and hold on!

🍁 River tackle for smallmouths should consist of a spinning rod and reel anywhere for 6-7' in length with 4-10 lb. test line. Small jigs and lures along with worms, minnows, crayfish and leeches will be the top producers.

🍁 The best live bait rigs for river fishing are the three way drop sinker and Gapens bait-walkers. Because of the current and large rocks, a sliding rig gets caught up instantly.

🍁 Many of the streams and rivers that in the spring and fall draw steelhead and salmon will harbour schools of smallmouths during the summer months. Take an ultralight outfit loaded with 4 lb. test and a handful of jigs and grubs and go to a small stream near you. The larger pools will always hold some smallmouths.

🍁 Smallmouth bass aren't usually found deeper than 30', one reason for this is that there is an absence of crayfish past this depth. Smallmouth in many northern lakes have to adapt themselves to following certain baitfish schools in deeper water.

🍁 It's important to note that when jig fishing, try to balance your line weight and the weight of the jig to your particular technique. You may be drifting over rocky shoals, still fishing along weed lines, or even casting in a productive stream.

♣ When using frogs for smallmouths use smaller size frogs as Spring beepers and immature leopard frogs. Fish them below the surface with a sliding sinker rig in deeper water, and on the surface in shallower water.

♣ When fishing lakes with channel markers, try live bait fishing right by the marker buoys. Smallmouths will cruise up and down these deeper channels in search of food.

♣ If you snap off the claws of crayfish so they can't grab weeds, they will be less likely to crawl under rocks.

courtesy of Berkley of Canada

Fishing for Walleye

Walleye

courtesy of   Ministry of Natural Resources

Fishing for Walleye

COMMON NAMES: pickerel, yellow pickerel, dore, walleye

One of the number one sought after gamefish in Ontario is the walleye. Most fishermen will agree that for its eating qualities, texture and light flavour, this fish can't be beat.

Even though the term "pickerel" has been used for years throughout our Canadian waters, the U.S. identification "walleye" is here to stay. The term refers to an eye that turns outward, showing more than the normal amount of white and the Canadian pickerel certainly has prominent eyes. Their large glassy eyes serve them well, both for finding prey after dark and in the gloom of deep water.

The walleye is a "spiny-rayed" fish closely related to the perch. Being the largest member of the perch family, the walleye can reach a weight of over 25 pounds. The average walleye is around 3 pounds, yet in some parts of Ontario such as the Bay of Quinte, the average weight is about 5 pounds. Walleye prefer cooler water and are sensistive to bright sunlight. The most productive fishing times will be confined to the low light hours of the day. Night fishing is by far the most productive time.

Walleye are piscivorous, meaning feeding mostly on other fish. These delectable fish are either caught by still fishing, drifting with minnows or trolling, Walleye are a schooling fish and if you catch one, keep fishing the area, the odds are in your favour to keep on hooking more.

Fishing for Walleye

* You can locate pickerel in deep water all summer long. Use a flasher or graph to locate deeper water structure and vertical jig these areas with spoons, jigs and live bait. You may stumble on large schools of walleye that very few people ever fish for.

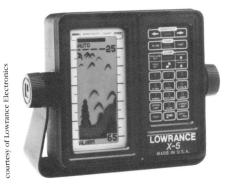

courtesy of Lowrance Electronics

* During late fall walleye will venture into extremely shallow water at night. They will roam in schools in search of frogs and other amphibians that are forced out of the marshes because of ice-up. It's at this time that walleye can be caught on surface lures in water 6″ to 3′ in depth.

* If you are looking for areas to fish walleye in late fall at night and in shallow water, creek mouths, boat channels and cattail shorelines are hotspots to try.

* A countdown method of fishing is great for walleye. For example, just cast your lure out and count to four or so, then start retrieving. If after awhile you don't get a strike, change your count until you hit the magic number. (see pier fishing)

* To locate shallow water walleye at night, listen for the "slurping" sound that they make when they are feeding on the surface.

* The best baits for shallow water surface fishing for walleye are twitching lures as the #II Rapala or Rebel wobbling minnow.

* When wobbling lures such as Rapalas and Rebels won't produce, switch to a spinner or worm harness and worm. Heavier spinning rigs as Earie Dieries work well both for trolling and drifting. These can produce fish when nothing else will.

* Anglers have found it easy to catch walleyes around sunken islands in early morning and late evening, but during the day they disappear. This is the time to fish the open waters just off the productive shorelines. You should be able to locate these same walleye suspended in open water.

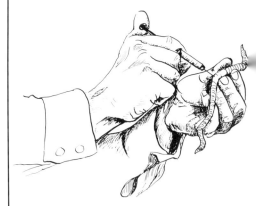

* Inject your dew worms with some air from a hypodermic needle. They'll be more buoyant staying just off bottom and will wriggle irresistibly for long periods of time.

HOW TO FISH IN AND AROUND WEEDS

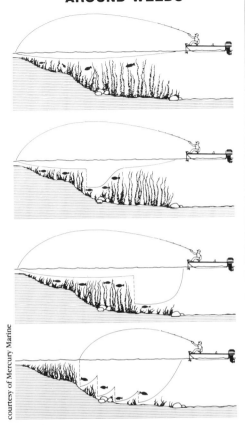

courtesy of Mercury Marine

🍁 If you are jigging near heavy weeds and you constantly get weeds on your jig try snapping your jig off the bottom, this will help you rip through the vegetation and at the same time letting your jigs drop in front of fish in a more natural way.

🍁 When using jigs for walleye, retrieve the jig after it touches bottom, reel in a little slack line while raising and lowering your rod tip. Repeat, let the jig hit the bottom. Depending on the area, this technique may be sped-up. However, generally slow is best. Other variations can be used for suspended walleye.

🍁 During spring, walleye are found in the shallow waters. The use of live minnows, worms and spinners off bottom work best. If you turn to using jigs, drag them also off bottom using a slow presentation.

🍁 It's been said that fathead minnows are an effective bait for walleyes, but for some unexplained reason the female minnows catch more walleyes. The females are usually more silvery and lack the bumps on the head. Shiners get the nod as the best second choice.

🍁 During the summer months, walleye can also be found in deep water off shoals and along weed lines. Most serious walleye hunters go after these fish at night due to their feeding habits, bringing them into the shallows.

🍁 Whether fishing from shore or in a boat remember, walleyes travel in schools. When you land one, work the area over, you should get into a few more.

🍁 The best type of rod for fishing walleyes is a medium or light-medium action spinning rod in the 7 foot length.

🍁 Trying to decide what jig to use for walleye sometimes is a problem. Keep these 3 things in mind: 1. weight of the jig 2. current force 3. line weight (thickness vs. pound test).

Fishing for Walleye

🍁 "Slower and slower" is the preferred presentation for walleye no matter what the season.

🍁 One bait that's lethal for walleye which is sometimes overlooked is leeches. Leeches work especially well in rocky, clear lakes and in fast water below dams. Drift the leeches right on bottom or use a floating jig to suspend them.

🍁 When fishing for walleye on bottom a sliding sinker works great. Thread a ¼ to ½ oz. egg or bullet sinker on your line, leave about a 16" lead and pinch on a splitshot to prevent the sinker from falling down to the hook, then add your hook to the end. This technique will allow the bait to stay where you want it, but when the fish starts to take line it won't feet any weight because the line travels freely through the sinker.

🍁 If you want more control of your bait while trolling use the "back trolling" method. You'll be able to move more slowly, and control your speed better as well as your lure.

Troll Direction

🍁 Walleye like cooler water (50 to 70 degrees). Their eyes are very sensitive to light therefore drop offs are the best place to look for them.

When trolling for suspended walleye you can use leadcore line, steel line, pink ladies and dipsy divers to help deliver your lures to the proper depths.

If you are fishing for suspended walleye and trolling isn't producing, try vertical jigging with heavy spoons ⅜ to 1 oz. in size. At times this will be the most productive method.

On some of our southern lakes such as the Kawarthas, walleye get used to the constant pressure of trollers. Try using planer boards with rapalas and worm harnesses in the areas that everyone is fishing, you may be surprised by the results.

If the walleye suspend in the lake you are fishing invest some money in a manual downrigger. You can fish two rods from one rigger and you can lower or raise your bait to any desired lepth.

If you are trying to bounce bottom trolling for walleye and you constantly get caught up, use a Gapen Baitwalker in ¼ to 1 oz. size and add a leader 12 to 24" in length. Use floating, wobbling lures and you will feel the difference and will get great results.

In the spring, walleye can be located in fast moving waters, such as waterfall areas, dams, river mouths and their inlets.

Walleye much rather prefer rocky or gravel bottoms. This type of bottom structure enables the fish to find food quite easily.

Many anglers have been having great success with jig/minnow combinations. Keep the presentation as slow as possible bouncing bottom.

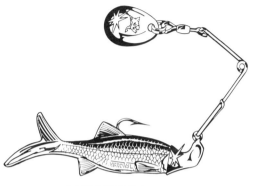

VIBROTAIL®
SPIN & MINNOW™

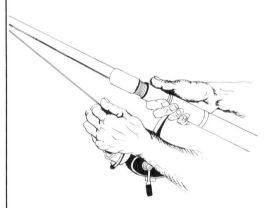

When walleye are finicky about biting, try holding the line just above your reel in your hand. You get to feel the bite almost immediately – then set the hook.

Very few people fish with frogs for walleye. In late fall walleye feed on frogs heavily. Next fall go to your favourite walleye spots and try fishing frogs on the surface and below as well.

Fishing for Walleye

Walleye in deeper water aren't affected as much by surface changes in temperature, weather and amount of light. If you are shallow water fishing and its not producing fish, go to those spots you have caught fish at in deeper water.

Some walleye will be attracted to wood or surface cover. If you walleye fish in a shallow lake don't overlook stumps or lily pads, at times these will harbour walleye as well as bass and musky.

If you are fishing new waters for pickerel, try these spots to find fish;

a) weed beds in the middle of the lake

b) points along the shoreline

c) bays along the shore

d) structure such as islands, humps, bars and deeper holes

One of the best techniques for catching walleye is drift fishing. Find some structure, weedline or shoreline and try letting the wind do the work. Drift with live bait or lures. On very windy days walleye can hold in certain areas in relationship to the wind and the only way to get to these fish properly is by letting the wind take you over them.

If you are trolling and pick up one pickerel, mark the spot. Blue Fox manufactures two great market buoys, one is designed to be seen in fairly calm water from a short distance, one is designed for larger waters and to be seen from a further distance.

courtesy of Normark

🍁 If you go to your favourite river to fish for walleye and they aren't there during the day try the same spots at night. Pickerel can switch to night feeding as well as daytime feeding and they will be attracted to very shallow water areas at night.

🍁 Shoreline fishermen can have some hot pickerel fishing at night. Pick a pier, dock or bridge and cast in the same areas, the odds are you will catch walleye randomly all night long. Pickerel will migrate many miles at night in search of food.

🍁 When you are fishing fast water for walleye cast your jig up into the current, this way you will have more jig control and you will be bouncing the jigs right in front of the fish.

🍁 When casting wooden plugs such as Rapalas in fast water always start by casting at 45 degrees across the river and allow the lure to work as it is taken down, then retrieve it against the current pausing it every 5 sec. or so. Most of the walleye will hit on the pause.

🍁 Many anglers like night-fishing for walleye. Make sure you have these few essentials along with the rest of your equipment: hand lantern, bug spray and an anchor rope. If you're in a boat, you'll need life jackets and proper boat lighting.

🍁 Walleyes have been known as short striking fish. They tap and nip at all kinds of bait. Like many species, the best tip here is to afix a trailer hook to the end of your lure or bait and your success rate should go up.

Fishing for Walleye

* Many walleye fishermen don't realize that you can troll successfully with jigs. Trolling at slow speeds gives you total boat control and you can cover a great deal of water very effectively.

* Most people assume walleye are always on the bottom of the lakes. This is not always the case. In most northern lakes during the summer months walleye will suspend above and below the thermocline. It's at this time that they will migrate following schools of herring all summer long. Deep diving crankbaits trolled 50-200' behind the boat will work best.

* Walleye are night feeders therefore that's the best time to fish for them. Try using a black light instead of a bright flashlight. Flourescent lines illuminate sometimes up to 75'. Using this type of high visibility line will enable you to visually see the strike before you feel it. The other bonus is that the light diminishes several inches under the water surface.

* Water temperature in the spring is the key factor with walleyes. If snow and cold temperatures keep the water temperature chilled the walleye spawning instincts will be stalled until conditions are right.

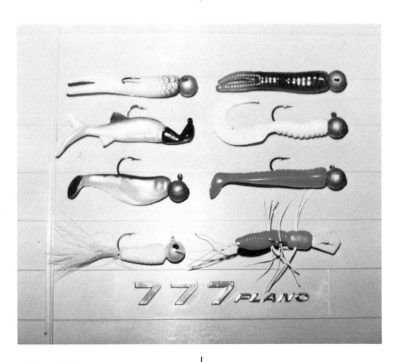

* Many walleye fishermen use different coloured twisters for pickerel. They work all season long at all depths. Yellow, white, black and pearl are the most popular colours.

* Walleyes can almost always be found right near lake bottom no matter what the season. The only difference may be the structure and/or depth.

❧ Minnows are a great walleye bait. Try snipping the tip off you minnow's tail. He'll have difficulty staying upright and therefore will move about more, attracting other fish.

❧ When fishing worms on bottom for pickerel, add a piece of styrofoam in front of the hook to keep the worm off bottom or use a floating/ neutral buoyancy jig. This will help you from constantly getting caught up and will produce more fish.

❧ When jigging for walleye with rubber, maribou or bucktail jigs tip the jigs with a minnow or a piece of worm. Once the walleye gets close enough to the lure they will be convinced into striking.

❧ When you bag a walleye, pay close attention to where it hit, what type of current your lure was in and the speed of your retrieve. By duplicating the original presentation, you should be able to land more walleye.

❧ When drift fishing for walleye, it's important to keep your rod tip down and slightly to one side, so that you can set the hook when you feel a tap. If you miss a strike put the rod tip down again and stop your retrieve, the feeding walleye may strike again.

❧ If someone says "jig and pig", you normally think of bass, especially largcmouth. Believe it or not, these rigs are deadly on walleye. Just dress your twin tail or pork leech on your favourite jig and spinner and see for yourself.

❧ Here's some tips to predict where walleye can be found according to their seasonal migrations;

1) Spring - Look to shallow water areas for walleye. Rocky shorelines, shallow weed beds, creek and river mouths and fast water areas will hold walleye right after apawning.

2) Summer - The walleye may be found throughout a particular lake. By this time they will be drawn to deep water structure, deep weed beds and weed lines. Though some pickerel will be found in shallow water as well, most walleyes will travel the shorelines at night. Fast water areas aren't as productive through the summer and will draw mostly smaller fish.

3) Fall - The walleye will again be drawn to shallower water and especially fast water areas. The deeper water will still hold walleye, but the best fishing is found around shorelines, islands and shallower water structure from 6-15'.

❧ Fish the water 2-10' in depth at night or early morning or late evening. During bright sunlight, fish the adjacent deeper water 10-20'.

courtesy of Berkley of Canada

Muskie and Pike Fishing

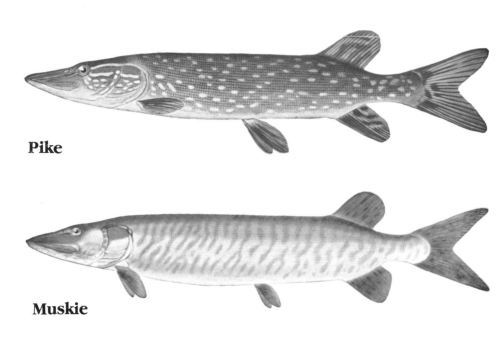

Pike

Muskie

courtesy of Ministry of Natural Resources

Muskie and Pike Fishing

COMMON MUSKIE NAMES: maskinonge, muskellunge, lunge, muskie

Many versatile anglers have never hooked a muskie, properly known as the "maskinonge". On the other hand, they've probably had many follows and didn't know it.

The sly muskie will routinely follow a lure to the boat, giving the angler a frightful scare, turning at the boat, forming a good-sized swirl and then slipping back into his favourite feeding grounds.

The muskie is often confused with the northern pike, but it can be distinguished by the lack of scales below the eye on both cheeks. In comparison, the cheeks of a pike are fully scaled.

Muskie spawn about 2 weeks after the northerns do. They will migrate in open water or travel up small streams and creeks. The muskie is a much stronger fighting fish than the pike.

Once hooked it may run for yards, often jumping high out of the water while trying to shake the hooks free. Muskies prefer slightly colder and deeper water than pike. The "muskellunge" are also known as solitary fish and will cover large areas in search of food.

Without a doubt, the muskie is the most prized freshwater gamefish. Known for its aggressive strikes and spectacular, aerial acrobatics. It can cut or even snap conventional monofilament lines with ease.

Even though these fierce fighters are much like the well-known pike, muskies are still Canada's largest freshwater fish. Many can grow over 65 pounds, yet the average fish caught is between 5 to 10 pounds. Muskies in the 40 to 50 pound range are caught annually in Ontario. The world record is just over 69 pounds landed by an angler trolling in the St. Lawrence River.

COMMON PIKE NAMES: *northern, grass, jack, great northern.*

Northerns are frowned upon by anglers because they find smaller fish easier to catch. However, most of these fishermen have never caught a fish over 12 pounds.

Northerns are probably the most vicious warm water gamefish. They will wait along weed beds or other cover for passing prey and attack it unexpectedly.

Pike will live in any shallow water bays and drop-offs close to dense vegetation. Their diets vary from minnows, frogs, snakes, and crayfish to even other pike.

They do spawn earlier than muskies, in fact as soon as the ice melts. At this time the eggs are laid on vegetation or silt bottoms along shallow waters.

Pike prefer quiet, weedy waters 2 to 10 feet in depth. Trolling, live bait fishing and casting are among the most productive methods for northerns. Among many effective lures, "daredevils" standout as the most famous. Early morning is the best time to catch these fish. Smaller fish may be easier to catch, but hook a lunker and you've got a battle on your hands.

courtesy of O.F.A.H.

* Fishing late fall for pike and muskies will definitely produce larger fish. These fish will feed very heavily to prepare for the cold ice-over period.

* Muskies are usually solitary and territorial in their habits and a large area must be covered in order to locate them.

* Muskie have a limited range and will stay close to their homing grounds which host weedbeds, drop-offs, even rock bars.

* Whenever you hook a musky, you should try to land it as soon as possible. Musky, when exerting pressure, as running and jumping, get a lactic acid build-up in their bodies. After they are released, because of this acid build'up they could become paralyzed and die.

* Lymphosarcoma is a common cancer found in muskies throughout Southern Ontario. If you catch a musky with one or more open sores on it's skin, don't eat it. Release it and report it to the nearest Ministry of Natural Resources office. Not much information is known on this disease, therefore, the Ministry recommends not eating these fish.

* Since these particular fish have bony mouths, you may find that single hook lure will work better. Generally speaking, it's easier to sink only one hook in over the barb than three.

Muskie and Pike Fishing

* The best muskie spots in most lakes are along weed lines adjacent to deep water or near lake inlets, stump or log areas. Any points extending out into the lake are also worth a try.

* When live bait fishing for musky or pike, always wait for these fish to swallow your bait. Musky and pike will take quite a while to turn a baitfish around in it's mouth, before it swallows it.

* Pike strike in a different way than most other gamefish. They will wait near weeds for an unsuspecting fish to swim past, then charge out and attack it from the side. After crushing its prey, the pike slowly turns the fish and swallows it head first.

SUPER VIBRAX™
DOUBLE BUCK™

* Big flashy spinners are readily taken by both muskies and northerns throughout North America and at different times of the year. Cast or troll them near structure, shorelines, or weed beds.

🍁 Muskies will fight much harder than pike. Once hooked they can dash wildly, often jumping high out of the water in an attempt to shake the hooks from its jaws. Failure to have control over the fish at this time, or to keep a tight line usually means loosing the fish.

🍁 The chief food for muskies is other fish, don't be afraid that the lure you are using is too large, the larger the better.

🍁 It seems a shame to see a good pair of pliers become sticky and unuseable. Just place them in a pair of old jeans and run them through the washing machine. When the cycle is finished, they'll work like new. Now all you have to do is keep them oiled.

🍁 Any of the larger spoons of the "daredevil" type will produce pike anywhere, anytime. Silver, red and white ones are the most popular.

TOR-P-DO SPOONS™

🍁 An easy method to store long wire leaders is to coil them together and then use a garbage bag tie to hold them in place.

🍁 If you have a muskie or pike follow your lure to the boat, don't slow down your retrieve. Instead, reel faster just to change the action of you lure, it just may trigger the "big one" to bite.

Muskie and Pike Fishing

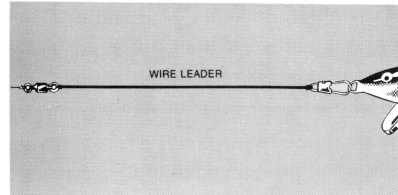

WIRE LEADER

courtesy of Normark

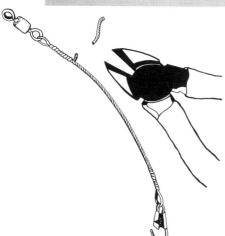

🍁 Northern pike are great for eating, but should be skinned and have their Y bones removed.

🍁 Pike tend to hang inside weed beds, whereas, musky most often cruise the outside edge.

🍁 Flats located at river and creek mouths are ideal areas to look for musky and pike.

🍁 On many northern lakes vegetation is sparse. On these lakes troll the shorelines with Rapalas, Rebels and other large musky plugs and cast to any points, deep bays or islands.

🍁 Terminal tackle is very important when fishing these heavy-toothed fish. Use a wire leader to help prevent break-offs (Lost Fish!)

🍁 The musky prefers slightly colder water than the pike and should, therefore, be fished in more open waters of the lake rather than in weedy bays.

🍁 To find productive fishing areas for northern pike, look for cold water springs in lakes and large rivers during hot summer days. Springholes in the ice during the winter will give you clues to where to look during the summer months.

🍁 Leaders are a must when musky or pike fishing, use extra long leaders for best results. These fish tend to roll in the line when they are being fought. If the leader isn't long enough the line may go over the fish's gill rakers and get out.

🍁 Styrofoam coolers make great storage tackle boxes for large muskie and pike lures. Just hook the last treble hook on the cooler lip edge until it's used again.

* When you locate small fish such as perch, sunfish and rockbass you should in turn find large predator fish, like the pike and muskie. These are their favourite forage food.

* When choosing musky and pike plugs, choose plastic or glass plugs over wood. Pike and musky can inbed their teeth into wood and when you set the hook nothing happens. With a hard-finish plug, when you go to set the hook the plug will slide in between a fish's teeth until the hooks penetrate.

* More and more fishermen are releasing trophy muskies and pike. Remember, the less you handle your catch the better. Since unhooking the lure sometimes becomes a difficult task, take hold of the fish by the head with your thumb and forefinger in the eye sockets – not the eyes. The other fingers should be pressed firmly against the skull bone, remove the hook and place the fish in the water. Grasp your catch by the tail and hold it in place until it has enough strength to swim away on its own.

* Don't be fooled all the time. Big fish sometimes go after smaller lure than you think. Try using ⅜oz. twister or vibrotail jigs. You'll be surprised how mnay 10 to 15 pound class fish you'll hit on.

* Large suckers, 8 to 14 inches make an ideal baitfish for muskie and pike.

Muskie and Pike Fishing

courtesy of O.F.A.H.

🍁 Trophy northerns and muskies will be found suspended in water 15-40' deep close to major structure, weed beds, or shorelines.

🍁 Keep in mind that most Provinces and States have a size limit on musky. In Ontario the minimum size limit is 28" in length.

🍁 If you're using premium monofilament line, make sure you use at least 25 to 30 pound test. You may want to try dacron line if your hook sets are missing; it has less stretch than monofilament.

🍁 Muskies have very hard bony mouths so when they hit, set the hook hard to make sure the barbs are embedded.

🍁 Motor noise from your outboard may attract northern pike and muskies. Try some speed-trolling next time with about 25 to 40 feet of line directly behind the boat. It seems as though the prop wash and water agitation stimulates these monster-fish to come in close to the boat and strike a lure.

🍁 Jerk baits like the Suick are floaters. The angler's rod has to provide the action for the lure. The suick utilizes a rear metal fin and downcurved head to drive it underwater when it is jerked. Use a pumping motion, pull - reel in slack line - pull, etc.

🍁 Northerns will usually be found in higher numbers than musky in shallow water. Many northerns can move in and occupy a weed bed, whereas, only one or two muskies will move into the same type of weed bed.

❧ A styrofoam cooler or pail is used by many musky fishermen to store large musky and pike plugs. Just remove the lid, drape your plug inside and pierce the last treble on the top inner edge.

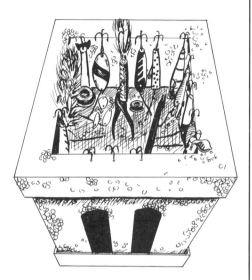

❧ Don't be surprised when fishing tight cover for bass. You just may hook into a 8 to 15 pound northern off a reed line. They too like the protection from the sun.

❧ Remember muskellunge like the faster moving lure than the northern pike. When trolling for "musky" increase your speed off deep weedlines.

courtesy of O.F.A.H.

❧ In clear water, large muskies tend to go into the deeper depths of the lake. It seems as though no lure is too big for a trophy muskie.

Muskie and Pike Fishing

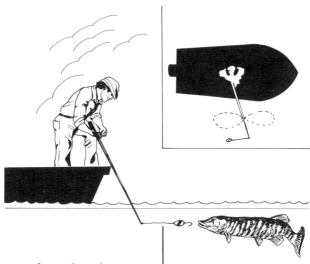

❧ Different types of wooden plugs jerked through the water close to the surface are great musky and pike baits all season long.

❧ If you want to cover a lot of water are fast – use a white or chartreuse spinnerbait. If a pike is feeding, he'll most certainly go after your bait if the presentation is right.

❧ The fall months have always been exceptional for muskie fishing. You should keep an eye on your lure throughout every cast and retrieve. If you think you see a follow, don't stop your lure, speed it up a bit and when it gets to the boat maintain a figure 8 pattern for a bit. It just may entice the monster to hit.

❧ When trying to remove a line from a pike or muskie and you don't have pliers, always jam the mouth of the fish open with a large lure or even a stick, then proceed to remove your lure. This precaution may save your hands from some sharp cuts and scrapes.

❧ In shallow water areas, you may see a muskie lurking along a weed line. Keep casting around him – he may surprise you and himself when he strikes your lure.

❧ If you prefer to troll for muskies, speed up your boat to twice the speed you would normally use for any other fish.

Fishing Trout in Rivers, Streams and Inland Lakes

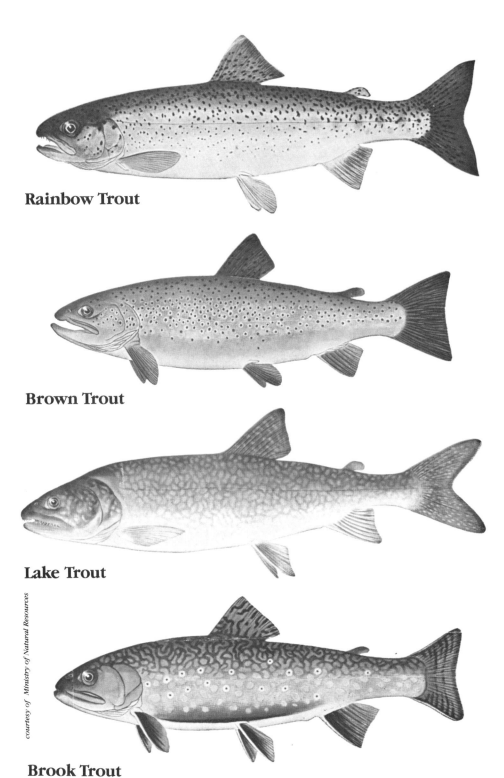

Rainbow Trout

Brown Trout

Lake Trout

courtesy of Ministry of Natural Resources

Brook Trout

Fishing Trout in Rivers, Streams & Inland Lakes

COMMON SPECIES: rainbow – steelhead, brown, speckled – speckies, lake

Grouping river and steam fishing is a difficult task due to the great variety of techniques and freshwater species available to the angler. Therefore, in this chapter we've isolated mainly on the trout species.

Probably the most majestic looking trout is the steelhead. Known by many fishermen as a hard fighting fish that is capable of long runs, magnificent jumps and a fish that "just won't stop fighting".

The fish is native to the west coast, but has been introduced to many rivers and streams throughout Canada. Steelhead spawn in the spring and fall. It's at this time that river fishermen get great opportunities to hook these fish.

During the early life of a steelhead, they will feed on all kinds of aquatic insects, crayfish, worms and minnows. Once the fish reaches adulthood, they migrate to a major body of water such as the Great Lakes or salt water. Here they feed exclusively on herring, alewife and smelt growing up to 30 pounds, even though the average fish weighs 3 to 8 pounds.

Catching these fish when they are spawning is very specialized task. Normal food is usually ignored at this time. Spawn sacks the size of a dime consisting of trout or salmon eggs tied in a fine netting are the most popular stream bait. Spinners, plugs and spoons also work well when trying to make steelhead strike.

Fishing Trout In Rivers, Streams and Inland Lakes

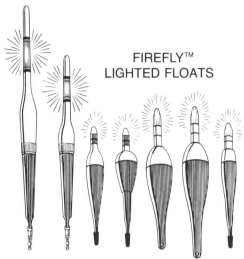

FIREFLY™
LIGHTED FLOATS

❦ Pools with spooky steelhead can be fished successfully at night with the aid of a "night float". Blue Fox makes a variety of lightweight floats which are powered by a lithium battery. Fishing at night may be the only way to catch these fish and the odds are good of catching some brown trout as well.

❦ If the water is high and dirty, fish the head and tails of pools first. Drift close to bottom and try to cover as much water as possible with every drift.

❦ If the water is low and clear fish the pools and the middle of deep runs. Try changing to a float and eggs technique and fish at various depths.

❦ Dams and other obstructions will stop and hold steelhead for weeks or months. Most large pools on any of the rivers and streams in Ontario that have runs of steelhead will have "hold-over" trout. Some steelhead will remain in the rivers most of the summer. These fish have surprised many trout fishermen. These "hold-over" steelhead will feed actively and if not spooked will hit almost anything that comes near them.

Fishing Trout In Rivers, Streams and Inland Lakes

* During early season, fish protected pools where the current is slow. These spots usually show up in stream bends right after some fast shallow rapids.

* At many times throughout the year trout just gorge themselves on freshly-hatched insects. If all you own is a spinning rod and reel you can get into some fine action as well. Add a plastic bubble approximately 3 feet ahead of your little fly and you'll not only get extra casting weight but you will rarely spook the trout.

* When using a float and roe drifting technique remember to match the float to the various conditions;

  1) Low, Clear water - Use a very small float such as a porcupine quill or a tapered English style float. Use minimum shot and very small hooks. The light floats will move most natural in slow water (recommended weight - 4-8 BB shot)

  2) Faster water - Go to a larger float and weigh it down. This will slow down your drift so that your bait is suspended in one spot for the longest period of time, while looking natural (recommended weight - 3-5 0/7 shot)

  3) Large Rivers - Large float, heavier line (recommended weight - 3-5 0/3 shot)

* When it comes to choosing good colours for steelhead floats, chartreuse tipped floats are most visible under low light conditions such as early morning and late evening. Black floats with fluorescent orange tips are most visible in bright sunlight.

* Small garden worms fished with small hooks and light line will draw strikes when nothing else works.

Fishing Trout In Rivers, Streams and Inland Lakes

* For steelhead use a longer rod with light line. Most steelhead rods are 9½ to 13' in length and are made of fiberglass, graphite or boron materials. Line weight varies from 2 to 10 lb. test depending on the water conditions.

* Use the smallest hooks possible so they are most invisible (no. 10-18 trout hooks) and bury the hook in the bait you are using.

* Salmon eggs, trout eggs and worms are the most productive baits you can use to drift fish for steelhead in streams and rivers.

* Lil' Corkys and Blue Fox's new Dr. Juice bait float juicers are small styrofoam balls that look like a salmon egg. Place these on your line above the hook. They will slide back and forth and will work to attract fish and to keep the spawn sack off the bottom.

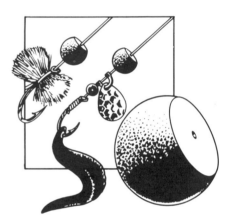

JUICERS™

BAIT FLOAT JUICERS™

* Spring steelheaders will catch ripe female trout, but end up losing most of the eggs when carrying the fish. Always keep a sewing needle in your fishing vest and sew the vent closed with monofilament line to ensure no loss of eggs.

* Many time, fish are concentrated in fast run pools of water. A better method than just casting and retrieving is current drifting. Just attach a minnow-like lure, even a spinner to your line with a few spitshots about 2 feet in front. Cast near the top of the pool and let the fast water catch your fish.

* You can increase your catch by crossing over and fishing the opposite shore. Not only are some sides easier to fish but can also protect you from spooking holding fish.

Fishing Trout In Rivers, Streams and Inland Lakes

❧ Cheese rolled up in the shape of an egg and canned sweet corn are good replacements for trout and salmon eggs.

❧ When approaching a pool, throwing in a handful of single eggs before drifting will increase the odds of hooking a steelhead immediately.

❧ A piece of bright yarn in fluorescent orange or yellow colours placed on the hook above a spawn sack can make the difference between getting strikes and not getting strikes in dirty water.

❧ One of the easiest ways to land an exhausted steelhead is either to beach it or to tail it with a 100% wool glove. Normark's fillet glove is also excellent to grab a fish with.

❧ Always approach a potential holding spot for fish from downstream. The fish will be lying with their heads pointing upstream and in turn will spook less readily.

❧ Dawn and dusk are prime time for steelhead. During rainy, overcast days steelhead fishing will be good all day long.

❧ The best time to fish for steelhead is after 2 or 3 days of heavy rain. As the water starts to drop and clear the steelhead will stop running and will hold in pools. This is when they are most active.

❧ Ideal visibility for steelhead fishing is 6″ to 1½′ below the surface.

❧ Use smaller spawn sacks in clear water and larger sacks in dirty water.

❧ Try to use the lightest float you can when drift fishing. The resistance of heavier floats will chase any potential takers away.

Fishing Trout In Rivers, Streams and Inland Lakes

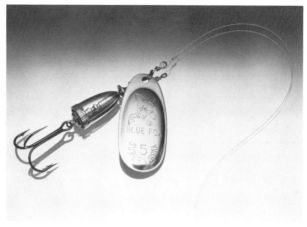

NEW SUPER VIBRAX BY BLUE FOX TACKLE

* If plugs don't produce, try an assortment of spinners. Vibrax, Olympic, Mepps and Panther Martin spinners are some of the most productive in silver, gold and black.

* When steelhead are spawning they will dig a "red". These "reds" appear as light patches of gravel between 1-3' in diameter. If you notice these light coloured areas, look for fish on the reds just above and below. Spawning fish can be very exciting to tease into striking.

* During the fall when salmon are spawning in the streams and rivers, always drift immediately below these fish. The odds are there are steelhead eating up eggs just below.

* Small minnows are always deadly for trout in the early season. Hook the minnow lightly through the lip and lob it gently and let it do its trick. When you feel something, wait, give that fish an extra second and then set the hook. You'll lose a lot less minnows and bag yourself a lot more fish.

* It takes some practice to read moving water and where the fish are. Try fishing undercut banks, points, bridge abutments, fallen trees even large rocks.

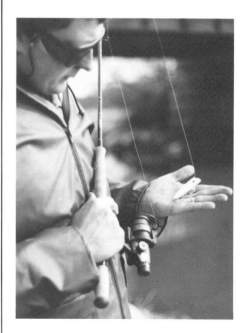

* Always wear high polarized sunglasses when steelheading, they will aid you in distinguishing water depth and will also enable you to spot fish.

Fishing Trout In Rivers, Streams and Inland Lakes

◆ If you fish rivers and streams in cold temperatures a lot, try using rubber-type gloves. They not only keep your hands warm but you can still bait your hooks and feel the hits.

◆ Instead of attaching your splitshot to your fishing line, add an additional piece of line as in the diagram. If your splitshot wedges between some stones or boulders, a tug may strip your weights but you'll still get your rig back.

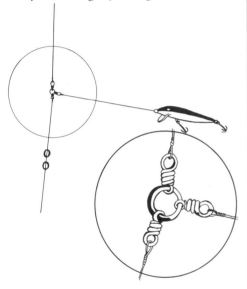

◆ When fishing pools with many holding steelhead use as small a hook as possible. This will decrease the chances of foul hooking fish and will still give you good hook sets.

◆ Don't use a steel leader when trout fishing. You don't need one because most trout don't have teeth big enough to cut your line and they will probably see it and you'll get less strikes.

◆ Most trout like cooler water, look for deeper pools, or springs entering a stream. These areas can hold a concentration of fish.

◆ Most stream trout will feed on all kinds of insects that fall into the water as well as crayfish, frogs, worms and minnows. All these work well when live bait fishing.

◆ Many trout fishermen pass up the best spots in the stream because they're too hard to get to. By using a longer rod and a flipping technique (see largemouth bass) you will be able to get all these fish-holding spots.

◆ For something different, try casting your fly onto the bank and pulling it into the water when fishing for trout. Throughout the day, trout spend part of their time waiting for insects under overhanging banks.

Fishing Trout In Rivers, Streams and Inland Lakes

❀ When trying to locate steelhead in a river or stream it's very important to learn to read the surface of the water;

1) **Slick water** - Usually means an even bottom, shallow and that it will hold fish when the water is discoloured or high.

2) **Rapids** - Marks the head of a run or pool, may indicate a sharp drop in depth. These areas can hold steelhead at any time.

3) **Slow Below Rapids** - Indicates a pool area, the water will be deeper here and steelhad will hold in these areas when the water is clear and low.

Tail End of Pools - This will be found where the deeper water turns to slick water, these are areas that steelhead use to spawn and can be extremely productive in the spring time.

❀ A wide range of flies work well for trout, especially during early morning and late evening. Just "match the hatch".

❀ When wading in a trout stream, try walking with the current and at the same time turn over rocks and logs. This will dislodge all types of food that will be carried down stream to waiting fish preparing them to take your offering.

❀ In small lakes try locating a beaver lodge. The branches usually provide plenty of cover for both minnows, crustaceans, invertebrates and trout.

❀ The best way to fish a small lake for trout is by using a boat and casting towards the shore attempting to find holding areas.

Fishing Trout In Rivers, Streams and Inland Lakes

❧ Whenever approaching a trout stream, always keep a low profile to the land and if you can, cast your bait in before you get too close to the edge. Trout have very good vision and by using the surface of the water they have a window to see not only the surface but also onto the bank.

❧ During the spring when a lake is very cold, lake trout will stay close to the surface, so fishing for them by trolling a flat line can be very productive.

❧ Use natural coloured meshing in clear water. Spawnee Netting in yellow, white, orange and pink work best.

❧ Silver Williams Whitefish and standard Williams are first choice spoons by lake trout fishermen. Canoe type spoons are the second most popular type.

❧ Skeened trout eggs treated with powdered borax will smell stronger and will turn a deep orange colour. When the skeens become firm, pieces can be torn off and placed directly on the hook. In clear water nothing looks more natural than skeened eggs.

❧ Nylon stocking pieces will definitely hold your roe. However, if you substitute hot orange and pink nylon netting for the stocking material you'll be amazed at how many more strikes you'll get. Colour contrast to a trout are very important.

❧ All trout species are very smart and alert in their home waters. Try to use the lightest possible fishing line. You need every advantage you can get.

Fishing Trout In Rivers, Streams and Inland Lakes

❦ Brown trout are the most difficult to catch out of the other species. Fish for them when the water is discoloured after a rain or at night.

❦ One of the best-kept secrets for steelheaders is purchasing ladies light nylon scarfs in bright colours. Use them for tying trout and salmon eggs, the spawn sacs look brighter than being tied in any other material and are most visible in dirty water.

❦ When fishing with nymphs or grubs try to make short casts. Your bait will stay on your hook longer, stay alive longer and be able to be controlled through the pool more easily.

❦ Take your spawn tying material when you go steelheading, nothing can beat catching a female steelhead and tying the fresh eggs on the spot and using them.

Fishing Trout In Rivers, Streams and Inland Lakes

❧ Undercut sections of banks as well as fast water below a dam should provide plenty of action.

❧ Jigging for lake trout with a bucktail jug and minnow or strip of fish can be very productive over the summer months. Look for drop-offs and other structure in water 50-300' in depth and try drifting or vertical jigging.

❧ During the summer months when the water levels are down and clear, you'll catch more trout if you use smaller lures.

❧ When wading fast and/or deep water, use a wading staff to help maintain your balance. Remember to move slowly sideways to the current if you can. Here's where your fishing buddy can help, just walk arm and arm for extra balance.

❧ When still-fishing from shore for steelhead by using two Y-shaped sticks or metal rods you can make a very efficient rod holder that will keep your rod and reel off the ground, preventing them from being damaged by sand, dirt, etc. Push these into the ground until they are stable. Make your cast, then place the rod into the holders, leave the bail open and place a small pebble on the line to keep it taut. When a fish hits it will be able to take the line freely then just set the hook and hold on.

❧ When fishing bottom use some styrofoam in your roe bag to keep it suspended off bottom. This technique works extremely well when steelhead congregate at river mouths and when they are holding in large pools.

Fishing Trout In Rivers, Streams and Inland Lakes

◆ Lake trout feed mainly on herring in deeper water. Shiny spoons and plugs work well fished with leadcore line, steel line or with downriggers.

courtesy of O.F.A.H.

◆ By taking loose salmon eggs and boiling them until they become firm you can prepare single salmon eggs that can be fished on a hook without falling off. Single eggs together with light line can prove deadly in clear water.

◆ Ladies stockings and leotards are the most common materials to tie eggs with. Cut the materials into 2 x 2″ squares, place 3-6 eggs in the centre, lift up the corners and form a sac. Twist the top, tie off with thread and trim with a pair of scissors.

◆ If you catch a female steelhead and you have fresh eggs, the eggs will only last for a short period of time in the refrigerator before spoiling. There are several ways to preserve your eggs so that they will last for the fishing season.

1) Frozen eggs - Trout and Salmon eggs should be thoroughly washed in water, air dried on newspaper for about 15 min. and then should be placed in a glass, plastic or bag container. Try to remove as much air as possible before freezing them.

2) Salt Treating - Wash eggs and stir them in a brine solution made up of uniodized pickling salt and water. The more salt you use the tougher the shell of the eggs will become. Let the eggs sit in the solution from 2-15 days. Remove them, air dry them and store them in an air tight container in the refrigerator.

3) Borax, Borasic Acid - Eggs should be washed, air dried and sprinkled sparingly with either powder. Once they are completely covered place in an air tight container and refrigerate. If you choose, you can make a solution with these chemicals and leave the eggs in a bath.

◆ When drift fishing fast water areas, a small piece of sponge in the colour and shape of a spawn bag dipped in scent or oil can work better than real roe.

◆ When fighting a leaping steelhead dunking the rod into the water will create more drag and torque for the fighting fish and will surpress the rainbow from jumping.

Fishing Trout In Rivers, Streams and Inland Lakes

❧ Fish in the shallower waters when the river or stream is rising. Fish move toward the shallows to find food and escape fast currents.

❧ When using a float for steelhead you should always use a swivel below the float with a lighter leader attached to it. This will serve two purposes;

I) If you get caught up on bottom the lighter leader below the swivel will break and you will still have your float.

2) If a fighting steelhead starts to roll in the line, which they often do, the line won't get twisted because of the swivel.

❧ If the water is dirty and the fish are "shooting" rapids, switch to drifting bottom. Set the hook at the slightest twitch or snap, since the fish may hit very lightly at this time.

❧ By using food colouring you can colour trout and salmon eggs to whatever shade you prefer from gold to hot orange and pink.

❧ When storing treated eggs in the refrigerator add a few drops of Phenol to prevent mold and mildew over several months.

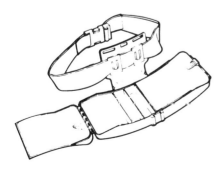

❧ If drifting eggs and worms don't produce fish, switch to casting plugs. Small flatfish, Kwikfish, fire plugs, tadpolys and hot shots work well to make steelhead strike. Black, silver, green and orange are the more productive colours. Fish these with the current and against the current. Fish them shallow and deep and vary the retrieve. At times these plugs will out-fish drifting baits.

❧ Steelhead run up rivers in the spring and fall. Most steelhead spawn in the spring but there are some fall spawning steelhead.

Great Lake

Fishing

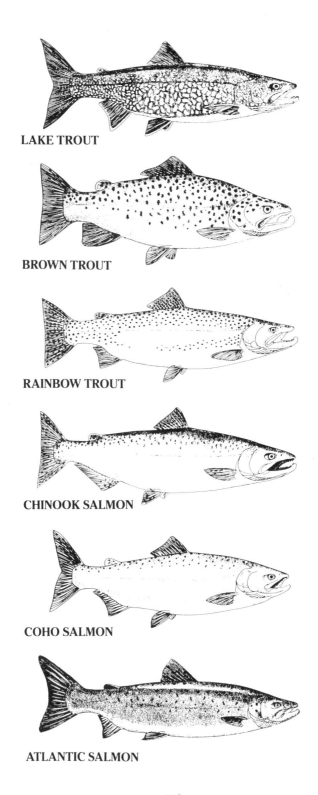

LAKE TROUT

BROWN TROUT

RAINBOW TROUT

CHINOOK SALMON

COHO SALMON

courtesy of Ministry of Natural Resources

ATLANTIC SALMON

Great Lake Fishing

COMMON SALMON SPECIES: atlantic, chinook (king), coho, pink

COMMON TROUT SPECIES: brown, lake, rainbow, speckled, steelhead

Todays angler has a variety of challenging gamefish to pursue. With over 9 salmonoid species available, it's no wonder that there's an obvious excitement about fishing the Great Lakes. Why has this fishing bug bitten so many people, so hard?

Is it the solitude, companionship or competitiveness? Maybe it is the abundant resources at our doorsteps, or is it the derbies promoting cash prizes up to a million dollars?

Whatever it is, it's a true challenge for any fisherman. Those of you who want to become consistent in catching salmon and trout in the Great Lakes must be familiar with the today's electronics and techniques.

Inhabitants of cold water, the main diet for the salmonoid species are the schools of alewife, smelt, herring and other small fish. Special fishing techniques have been used to catch them, especially in the mid-summer months where they are mostly found in fluctuating temperature zones called the thermocline. Downrigging is now a universal technique, used to catch salmon and trout consistently. Salmon have been caught close to 50 pounds yet the average runs from 10 to 20 pounds. Fishermen almost exclusively use clean-run spoons in a variety of colours behind the cannonball to hook the large variety of fish available to them throughout the Great Lakes.

The current sportfishing market has brought better boats and motors, nearly invisible fishing lines, and lures that duplicate real baitfish. Therefore, whether you fish from a boat, off a pier, or near a rivermouth, fishing the Great Lakes will be a more profitable experience if you take time to learn the facts that are included in this chapter

Great Lake Fishing

A fish diary is great for all kinds of fishing especially when fishing the Great Lakes. By tabulating such facts as the date, time of day, depth fished over, depth of lure besides its colour, size and tracking speed – you'll become a more consistent fisherman. For when the same conditions occur, you'll know what worked in the past.

Wait for sporting good stores to have sales on lures. You may not find the right coloured spoon but with a little paint and prism tape; you can design your favourite lure at one quarter the cost.

Compressed air has been used for years to clean cameras and lenses. A can costs about $5, and is a great device for cleaning your graph recorder and/or flasher, ridding it from dust, dirt and carbon.

Many salmon and trout are pretty good fighters and end up breaking your line by wrapping themselves into the line. It's a good idea to troll back over the area. You never know, your fish might be disabled in the entangled line right on the surface.

When smoke rises straight up expect no change in the weather.

Sportsmen who suffer from motion sickness can try using a product called "transderm V". It's a small disc that is stuck behind the ear and will work for several days. Although expensive, it's worth it.

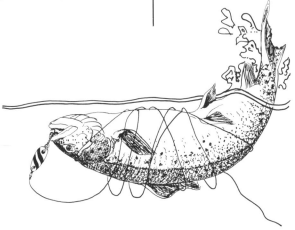

✤ In the spring, use a flat line technique (sometimes called a high line or surface line). By trolling jointed rapalas close to shore in either chartreuse, blue or fluorescent red you'll be able to have a great deal of success, maybe even more than charterboat operators.

✤ Try using a heavier cannonball when fishing deep or rough water. (10 to 12 lbs.) Many anglers try to skimp on small ticket items but for a few extra dollars your downrigger cable will bounce less in rough water and most importantly, track closer to the boat enabling you to pick up the weights on your graph recorder.

✤ Here's a good rule of thumb. The earlier or later in the day you fish from piers, the closer you should fish towards shore. As the sun rises, the salmon and trout will move out into the deeper waters. Overcast days will also hold the fish tighter to shore.

✤ In the Great Lakes, schools of salmon are often seen porpoising near stream mouths several weeks before they make their spawning run. They are actively feeding and always on the move. Being in shallower waters, they seem to spook quite easily and therefore, instead of trolling through and around these fish, stop, and try casting to them with spoons, action plugs even rapalas.

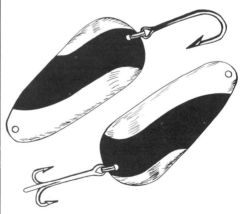

✤ Try replacing some of your lures with treble hooks to single hooks. You'll find that you'll lose less fish because the single hook will penetrate better when you set the hook. You will also be able to unhook your catch easier and release the fish without handling it too much and too long.

Great Lake Fishing

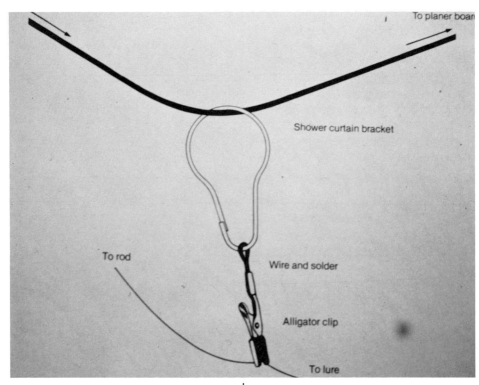

To planer boar[d]

Shower curtain bracket

To rod

Wire and solder

Alligator clip

To lure

🍀 A planer board release can be made quite easily by using an alligator clip and a shower curtain bracket. Remember to slip some thin rubber tubing over the tips of the alligator clip to help secure your fishing line. As in the diagram, secure the two by soldering.

🍀 Spring and fall are the best times to fish from piers. In fact, as soon as the ice is out and the water warms up a little, you can get a jump on the boaters.

🍀 Cannonballs and sinkers can be made quite easily from reclaimed shot which you can purchase from your local rod and gun club. Block lead takes longer to melt and the small shot is probably the cheapest source of lead you'll find.

🍀 Sometimes just a little extra flash on your spoons will trigger the elusive salmon to hit. Pick up a few different colours and experiment. You have everything to gain. Favourite colours to buy: chartreuse, blue and green.

PIXEE
SPOONS™

When you run out of releases an elastic band will work just great. In fact, many fishermen prefer using elastics; they do less harm to your fishing line and are certainly a lot less expensive. Pull one end of the rubber band through the other onto your fishing line. Pull it until it snubs tight and attach it to a snap swivel on your downrigger wire.

If you use crankbaits on your downriggers in early spring or late fall make sure you realize that they will dig several feet deeper than the downrigger ball setting.

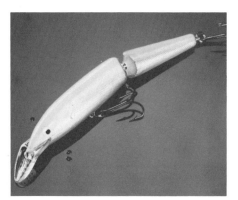

NEW SIZE JOINTED FLOATING RAPALA BY NORMARK

To help insure a good hook set, tighten your reel so that your rod tip will be bent downward as far as possible. By pulling the line by hand with one hand towards the reel, you can take up the slack quite easily with the other.

When fishing a large lake, especially Lake Ontario, make sure you have respect for the water. Watch the weather. A wind change can result in very rough water. Make sure your boat is of sufficient size to handle it or get off the water.

When a good-size salmon hits, it's wise to pull in other lines to eliminate tangles at boatside. Probably just as important, reel up your cannonballs so that they're out of the water. A wire cable touching your monofilament will surely cut your trophy loose.

115

Great Lake Fishing

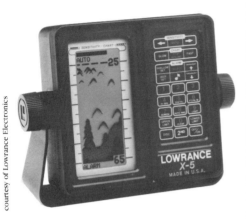

courtesy of Lowrance Electronics

🍁 Electronic depth sounders and graph recorders are important in that they indicate the water depth and type of bottom, schooling and individual gamefish, baitfish as well as bottom structures, shoals, etc.

🍁 If kinks develop in your downrigger wire, you may eventually lose all your releases including the cannonball if it breaks. Why risk it? Snip the line and splice it back together with proper crimps and it'll work like new. Eventually you may have to replace the entire wire line with a fresh roll.

🍁 If you want to keep your boat fresh and clean, purchase a quality good-sized cooler and mount it on your swim platform. Not only can you keep your fish on ice but you'll end up with more cockpit space – clean too!

🍁 Rubber squids occasionally mat up when they dry in your tackle box. Just drop them in a plastic baggie with a little talcum powder, shake it up and you'll shape them up and have them ready for the next dodger and fly combo.

🍁 When lifting a good-sized fish into the boat, raise the net on an angle to minimize the strain on your net handle. Most Great Lake fishermen like long and extended handles to help bring the big bruisers in without actually putting the boat into a neutral position.

🍁 Even in the hot summer months, early morning is a good starting place for cruising rainbows, browns and chinook salmon. They come into the shallows for baitfish and retreat to the deeper waters as the day goes on.

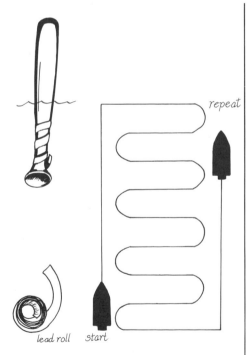

lead roll   start

repeat

* Before you spend thousands of dollars in fishing equipment for fishing the Great Lakes, go out on a fishing charter. Talk to the captain, see his up-to-date equipment and make sure what you are thinking of buying is necessary and in with the time.

KING AQUA
SPOONS™
(Single Sidewash Hook)

* A high visibility marker is very important when fishing the Great Lakes. You may want to pinpoint a group of salmon or baitfish and then troll in your favourite pattern. Here's a pattern that works almost every time.

* The principal food of most chinooks through the Great Lakes are alewife. Remember these preyfish run in different sizes at different times of the year. Try to match your spoons to the alewife size and you'll box more "kings".

Great Lake Fishing

❄ By purchasing hydrographical maps you'll be able to more easily locate long, sloping underwater points, submerged river channels, dropoffs, shoals etc. In the spring, these types of areas will generally hold more shallow-feeding salmon and trout because that's where the baitfish congregate and spawn.

❄ When using trolling boards make sure your outside lines are the farthest ones back behind the boat and the shallowest. The lure running inside of that one should have a shorter lead and run deeper. These tips will help prevent tangling when the fight is on.

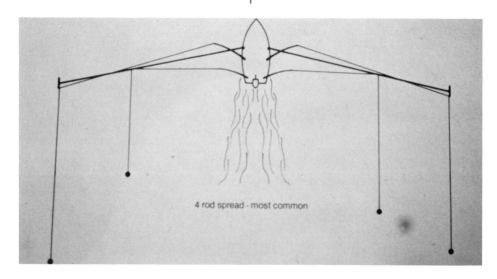

4 rod spread - most common

🍁 The four most important factors in fishing the Great Lakes are:

1. lure depth
2. lure speed
3. lure colour
4. lure size

←16"-20" long

trolling angle

🍁 You can easily make your own lure speed/trolling guide. Tie a line to a 2 to 5 oz. sinker to the side or stern of your boat. Note the angle at which your line is at when you get a strike on your rod. Whether you troll into the waves or with them, into the wind or not, you should be able to maintain a fairly close lure speed.

🍁 Various spoons and spinners as well as high speed trolling can put a nasty twist in your line, even with a quality swivel. Try using a lure that rotates in the opposite direction every so often. You can check the lure's rotation at the side of your boat before you attach it to your downrigger.

🍁 Temperature breaks such as dirt lines formed along river mouths, debris and algae lines out in deeper waters always host some salmon and trout action. The baitfish are located here and so are the predators.

HOW TO USE PLANER BOARDS FROM YOUR DOWNRIGGER

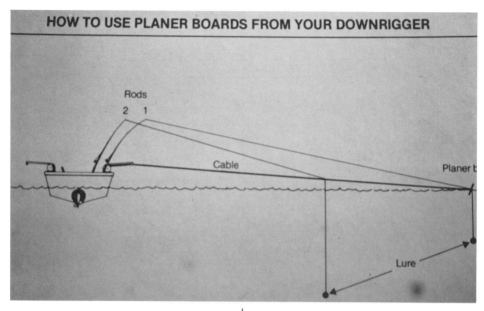

♣ If you are marking fish on your graph recorder and there are no takers at that particular depth, stagger several lines at varying depths and lengths from your cannonball until you find the magic combination.

♣ A good starting place when fishing open waters is other boats. When fishing is productive, a pack of boats form quickly however, be cautious when using planer boards. Getting too close may cause an unfortunate break-off, maybe a loss of a potential wall-hanging salmon.

♣ If you don't have a downrigger to get your lure down to the proper fishing depths, try using diving planers like a "pink lady" or "dipsy diver". The more line you let out, the deeper it will track. Many 20 pound plus salmon have been caught using this fairly inexpensive device.

♣ Many downrigger manufacturers will warrant their use with planer boards. Just turn your downrigger out at 90 degrees to your transom, attach your planer board to your release and let it go out to a 50 maximum width. This technique should be avoided in rough water. Be aware that the cable could break under heavy stress. However, this simple technique can still get your lure away from your boat's path when fishing is hot in the spring.

♣ Radios, both CB's and VHF are more than safety communication devices. You can get constant weather reports and valuable fishing advice like:

1. best lure of the day

2. best overall fishing depth

3. best trolling speed

4. the location of the hottest action on the lake.

♣ You can also use your downrigger in springtime shallow water fishing. After running out a long lead of about 100 feet or so, attach your fishing line to your release on the downrigger. Lower the cannonball a foot or two into the water. Tighten your rod into a heavy arc. Your rod is now set for action and a better hook set.

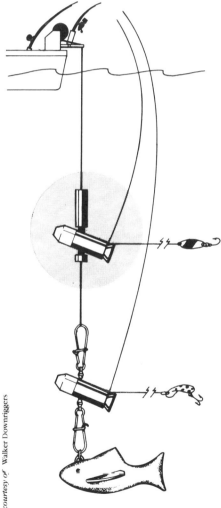

courtesy of Walker Downriggers

♣ Refrain from giving fish away, it usually ends up in the garbage. If you're not sure of the Ministry's guidelines for your catch, return the fish to the water so they can reproduce for the future.

♣ Downrigger cables, release clips as well as the fighting salmon can play havoc on your fishing line. Before each outing, infact throughout your excursion check for frayed, peeled or nicked line. The damaged line should be removed to insure line quality which in turn will help you land your fish.

Great Lake Fishing

courtesy of Walker Downriggers

❧ Trolling boards also called planer boards give the Great Lakes fisherman five major advantages:

1. he can cover a larger area of water

2. he can run more lines with a lot less tangles on turns etc.

3. lures remain away from the boats path and more in the fish strike zone area

4. he can get his lures into the shallows, even to 3 foot depths and not worry about hitting bottom with your prop

5. you can change lure speed with shorter turns

❧ You can make an inexpensive downrigger release by drilling a small hole in one of the legs of a spring-type clothespin. Just run your fishing ling through the hole, twist the clothespin a few turns and pinch this economic release to your downrigger cable.

❧ Water stratification sends salmon and trout into deeper waters during the hot summer months. By knowing your species preferable temperature zones; you'll more likely get into some action. Due to their size, power and derby prize structures, the chinooks are probably the most sought after salmon species. Look for them between 49 and 52 degrees F.

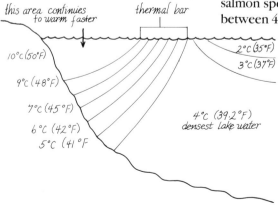

this area continues to warm faster

thermal bar

10°C (50°F)

2°C (35°F)
3°C (37°F)

9°C (48°F)

7°C (45°F)

6°C (42°F)

5°C (41°F

4°C (39.2°F)
densest lake water

🍁 Spring fishing for salmon and trout is always fun. Experiment to entice these fish to hit. Try different trolling speeds, use zig-zag or S-type turns as well as fishing in front of warm water outflows. All of these factors should increase your hits.

🍁 A stacker line does not necessarily need to be affixed to your downrigger cable 10 feet above your bottom set lure. By using a 4 foot (30 lb.) monofilament leader, adding two swivels and a spoon, you can drop this type of stacker to the belly of the line quite easily and effectively.

🍁 Many Great Lake fishermen are curious when it comes to knowing what depth the lure is actually at when they troll at different speeds. For example, if your cable is out at a 45 degree angle to the transom, you'll have to set your downrigger at 140 feet to actually get your lure down to 100 feet running depth.

🍁 Many anglers try to run a variety of spoons and plugs when searching for feeding salmon and trout. Remember many of these lures are designed by manufacturers to run at certain trolling speeds for ultimate action. Therefore, if you want to run a spoon and plug at the same time, make sure they are evenly matched.

Ice Fishing

Ice Fishing

Ice fishing is an enjoyable way to pass the winter months when other types of fishing are very limited. Undoubtedly, ice fishing has grown in popularity, like all types of fishing in the last decade. Ice hut operators have become successful in giving the average fisherman a winter treat in thousands of lakes throughout Canada.

Get to know the ice conditions, tackle and equipment that works and how to locate fish through the ice. You'll find ice fishing probably the easiest and most sociable type of fishing there is.

There are two variables; you'll need a lake with fish in it and sufficient "safe" ice on it to have some great winter fun. Many long-time ice fishermen have practically learned all the ropes. We've been able to pass on many of these hints, tips and specific techniques, that have made ice fishing as easy as one-two-three.

Besides safety, there'll be factors such as dressing for the cold, travelling across frozen waters, even appropriate seasonal techniques. Yet, one thing for sure, your initial cost will be very small and everyone will have the opportunity for some great winter fun. One thing for sure – your catch won't spoil!

Ice Fishing

🍁 A good way to warm up your hands and/or feet while fishing is to use bricketts and a coffee can. Just place a little sand in the bottom of the can and above that a layer of charcoal bricketts. The glowing coals will provide heat for hours. You may have to place a few holes in the can to stimulate air flow.

🍁 When you have drilled a number of holes for a weekend of ice fishing, remember to place a branch or twig in the unused hole. It'll save you time looking for it the next day and it'll be a safety measure in that you'll feel good about.

🍁 Always tip your spoons with minnows. Hook the minnow in between the eyes, pierce the fish through the bottom of the head and make sure the barb is exposed on top. When using a minnow tipped spoon you have to be careful you don't rip the minnow off by jigging too rough.

🍁 When ice-fishing waters with a current, use heavier weight to keep your bait down. The most common rig is a pickerel rig weighted down with a bell sinker.

🍁 For shallow water the best live bait rig is split-shot and a hook.

🍁 Small 1/16th ounce jigs are great for perch but you'll need larger ¼ ounce jigs for walleye and lake trout. You can even dress your jigs with minnows.

🍁 There are many ways to hook a minnow. One way is to hook your baitfish along one side of the dorsal instead of right through. The baitfish will remain alive longer as well as more active.

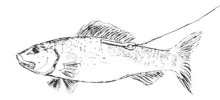

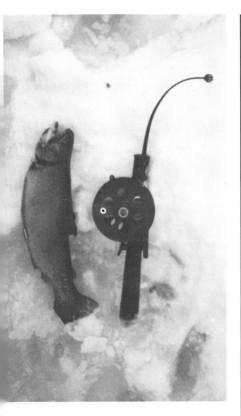

* If you are herring fishing and you start catching fish, fish as hard as you can while they are around. Herring travel in large schools and constantly roam. The fishing is usually fast and sweet.

* When trying to locate the herring, start jigging on the bottom then start walking back away from the hole while you are jigging. I use 10' intervals at a time, so as soon as you start catching fish memorize the depth and work that area thoroughly.

* The larger the auger diameter the greater the chance that the blades will slip when you are trying to cut a hole. Most ice-fishermen will agree that 6-8" diameter holes are plenty for most types of gamefish.

* When fishing for perch, pickerel, herring, speckles and smaller lake trout 6-10 lb. test is plenty strong. If you are fishing for Northerns, large walleye and trophy lake trout use 14-25 lb. test.

* Many people use heavier monofilament lines for ice-fishing because they believe the line gets stiffer and weaker in the cold. The line does get stiffer, but not weaker. Monofilament line is strongest in colder weather.

* Remember you can overchum an area. Pause ever 10 minutes or so to make sure you don't oversaturate your fishing hole. The current will also move some of the chum along the bottom.

Ice Fishing

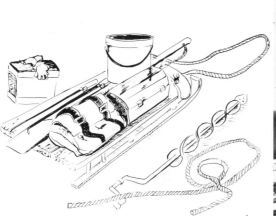

❦ Whether you go on foot or use a snowmobile, children sleds are great for hauling your equipment out onto the ice.

❦ When ice fishing an unfamiliar lake start with a triangle formation of holes about 50′ apart. You will cover more water and you will get a good idea of the water depth and vegetation, repeat this pattern until you find fish.

❦ Cautious ice fishermen will look for dark spots when venturing on the ice early and late in the season.

❦ When fishing in the winter a first-aid kit is a must, yet a survival kit would be better. Include these items in a small bag and you'll be surprised how many times you'll reach into the bag: handkerchief, wool socks, space blanket, zip-lock plastic bags, whistle, waterproof matches, instant tea or coffee, boullion cubes, granola bars, a few hard candies, piece of aluminum foil and a sharp knife.

❦ Take a gaff on your ice fishing trip if you own one. Some of the biggest fish are caught during the winter months and it would be a real shame to lose one at the rim of the hole.

❦ Many ice fishermen as well as winter steelhead anglers snip the thumbs and finger-tips from their gloves. This simple trick will allow you to manipulate your line rod and reel with very little difficulty.

✤ When ice fishing, it's best to snip a small piece of your live minnow's tail off. It will swim with a more erratic action that'll definitely draw more gamefish.

✤ Few people think of taking a flasher/fish finder on the ice, there are several portable models available for the dedicated ice fisherman. You can determine water depth, amount of vegetation on bottom and if any fish are under you without cutting a single hole. Simply clear the snow or slush off the surface of the ice and make sure the transducer has a solid contact with the ice surface.

✤ Never kill your minnows at the end of an ice fishing day. In the winter minnows can be kept alive in a garage, fruit cellar or basement for weeks if the temp. is cool and the water is changed occasionally.

✤ Extra holes usually pay off. When ice fishing, move your tip-ups around from hole to hole if they're not too productive. The best way is to cluster them in a more productive area such as deeper or shallower water.

✤ If you want to catch trophy lake trout in a lake with whitefish and lake herring. Catch some of the herring and use them for lake trout bait.

Ice Fishing

JIGGING ROD

NEW PANFISHER II ROD

PANFISHER ROD

THRUMMING ROD

🍁 For jigging most fishermen will use a short "ice-fishing rod". Normark has several models on the market designed for small fish right up to trophy Lakers and Northerns.

🍁 If your auger starts slipping check the blades for ice-up. Make sure to take a rag with you on the ice and wipe the blades carefully whenever you finish a hole.

🍁 Don't throw away dead minnows or injured ones. Freeze them and take them with you and use them to tip your spoons or jigs.

🍁 The most productive fishing areas are located near weedbeds, springs and where wind has blown away the snow, leaving just an ice surface.

🍁 Many winter fish travel in schools, therefore, it's often wise to have several ice holes cut together. Your tip-ups should fly up and down during their feeding frenzies.

✤ Remember when fishing for white fish; use an extremely sensitive tip-up and balance it on the stand and watch for the slightest movement, a bite may not just pull the line down, but may also be indicated by the line going slack.

✤ If you're able to clear the snow around the hole showing more ice, do so. The added light will help attract fish.

✤ Be careful when hooking your minnow. They can freeze very quickly. It's important that it is alive for maximum effect. Hook the minnow then hold it in your hand until you reach the hole, then slip the fish gently into the water, the minnow should try to swim away. Never let a minnow dangle in the cold air for long periods of time.

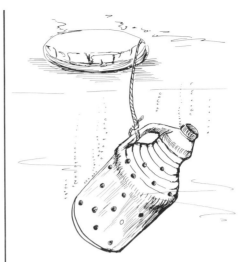

✤ A chum pot can be made quite easily from an empty bleach jug. Just drill ¼ inch holes in the jug, fill it with chum and hang it through the ice.

Ice Fishing

You can help your fishing success by chumming a hole. You can make chum up from a mixture of items, try these for a chum blend: pieces of worm, fish, bits of meat scraps all which should be ground up fine. Add some crushed egg shells even dry oatmeal and some gamefish should be around soon.

When going to smaller trout lakes make sure to check the fishing regulations, many smaller lakes have a "NO LIVE MINNOWS ALLOWED" law, but you can still use minnows as long as they are not alive.

Even walleye fishing in the winter is best at night. However, when it comes to pike, daytime is the best. Many ice fishermen leave too early, some of the best fishing occurs when it's too dark to see your flags.

Don't throw away your broken fishing rod. Save it and cut it down to 2-4' in length. Add a new tip to it and you will have an ideal ice fishing rod.

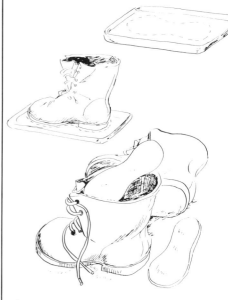

Heat-saving innersoles can be made quite easily from the foam plastic trays that meat is packaged on. Just trace an outline of your foot, trim the tray ends away and place them in your boots.

When necessary, before attempting to go out onto unknown ice thickness, cut a pole and carry it as if you were a tight-rope walker. If you crack through the ice the pole will prevent you from falling right through.

Many anglers use dacron braided line when ice-fishing at greater depth as for lake trout. They say the dacron line has less stretch and will hang much straighter to make it easier to determine when your lure or bait is on the bottom.

Drilling holes through the ice to check depths is tedious. With the use of an electronic depth sounder and a transducer you can save yourself a lot of work. Just place your transducer in a baggie with antifreeze, and then place it on top of the ice. Your depth reading should be quite accurate.

If you are fishing on ice covered with snow patches choose to make your holes on these snow patches. Fish in shallow water will sometimes use snow patches as cover and the snow will also provide better traction for running from hole to hole.

If you've never used an ice auger, you don't know what you're missing. Not only is the hole cut quicker, but you will have a nice even one without sharp edges. Besides if you want to cut a half a dozen or so throughout the day it'll give you more time to enjoy fishing.

First ice for almost all species is the most productive time to ice fish.

Dull auger blades can be steeled on the ice by using a pocket knife or portable steel, run the metal on both sides of the blades to bring the edge back.

Be careful never to drop your auger on the ice or road, the blades can become damaged very quickly and are expensive to replace. Always use a cover over the blades. To make one, take some rubber hose and slit it up the middle, make a hole at each end and run a large elastic through it. This will protect your vehicle and hands from getting cut.

For foot protection against the cold, wear 2 pairs of socks. Wear a light pair of cotton socks first with heavier wool socks on top. Cold feet are the first thing to ruin your fishing trip.

🍁 Here are some safe guidelines for going on ice of different thicknesses:

1-2" NO WAY

3" a few anglers spread out

4" general use

5" snowmobiles OK

8-12" cars and/or light trucks

🍁 A styrofoam cooler will help keep your minnows from freezing.

🍁 If you lose your ice-fishing ladle, borrow your wife's sieve. It will work well and you can return it to her clean and undamaged.

🍁 Many times a particular area on a lake can be productive for a number of weeks during winter. Mark your hot spot by placing a small branch or twig in your ice hole so that you can find the spot easy on your return.

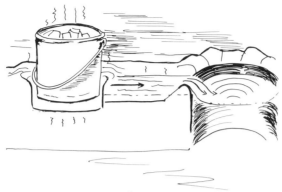

🍁 To keep your ice hole open in cold weather. Drill a second hole several inches deep next to your fishing hole. Place a large can of charcoal bricketts in the shallow hole. The warm water will circulate and keep it from freezing.

🍁 A portable flasher will enable you to know the lake depth before you cut your fishing hole through the ice. Can you imagine cutting a 2 foot hole over a shallow shoal? A topographical map will also help you if you are unaware of shoreline structure.

🍁 When ice fishing for lake trout try fishing at various depths, especially on bottom. Dead baits fished on bottom may produce some of the largest lake trout.

🍁 If you ice fish and don't have a hut to keep you warm you can stay warm by building a simple seat/heater. Use a wooden crate such as the ones used for holding pop bottles, invert it and attach it to a small sled or toboggan with hinges, inside place a catalytic heater. It will double over as an all-purpose storage box as well as a comfortable seat/heater.

🍁 Make sure that your fishing hole is free from rough edges of ice. If the edges are too irregular, your fishing line may fray and break while fighting a good-sized fish.

🍁 One of the best artificial baits for lake herring is rigging up a flashing spoon with a leader 6-10" long tied on to the bottom split ring where the treble was. At the end of the leader tie a small treble with a pearl attached to it. The spoon will resemble a herring chasing some food (the pearl), this gets other herring excited and active, making them strike.

Ice Fishing

❋ This winter, when the lake is frozen over, walk along the ice near the banks or road bridges which are fished in the summer from shore and look for lures hanging in the trees. You'll find plenty when the leaves are off the trees.

❋ When fishing 2 holes within a certain area on the lake, make sure you're not more than 60 metres from the nearest hole.

❋ Use the lightest line for perch (4 lb.) is just fine, (8 to 12 lb.) line for walleye and lake trout will also do the trick.

❋ When ice fishing for pickerel with live bait, if you see a bite, don't set the hook hard, just start bringing the line in with firm, steady pressure. Many times the walleye will close their mouths on the minnow and won't open it until they are flopped onto the ice.

✤ When ice fishing for speckles on an unfamiliar lake look for beaver dens. The brush piles around the beaver dens attract baitfish that in turn attract speckles. These piles will be found in water 6-12' deep and they may come right to the surface of the ice.

✤ Before using an ice spud or axe to make your ice fishing hole, attach a thin rope through the handle and around your wrist. This safety strap rig will prevent your tool from going to the bottom of the lake when you cut through your last section of ice.

✤ It's legal to use 2 hooks on one line. When ice-fishing use this to your advantage. Many times a fish will be lost on one minnow and then it will go for the second one. When using 2 minnows never pull up your rig immediately after losing the fish, wait 2 minutes and see if it will take the second hook.

✤ Chumming a hole actually attracts minnows and other baitfish. This in turn attracts the larger gamefish and that's what most anglers are actually ice fishing for.

✤ Baiting the hole that you will be fishing from will attract both baitfish and gamefish around that hole (cooked barley is a great chumming bait).

✤ Styrofoam or plastic pails are much better for holding your minnows than metal buckets. Metal buckets will ice-up in cold weather, whereas, the styrofoam ones won't.

✤ Cheap minnow buckets made of foam with rope handles have a tendancy to tear the foam where they are tied. To make one last a long time, pull the knot on the handle down 1 inch and wrap electric tape around the bucket a couple of times. Then all the weight is on the tape.

✤ For best results using minnows for ice fishing, hook the minnow through it's back in between the dorsal fin and the head, just above the back bone.

Ice Fishing

❀ When selecting lures for ice fishing here's some helpful hints:

(1) Walleye sometimes like slow moving lures in colder weather such as jigs and minnows, jigging Rapalas, other light spoons like The Williams woblers and flutter spoons. In milder weather they may change to striking fast dropping spoons such as the Mr. Champ, Alligator, Little Cleo and Rapalas Pilki spoon. Try sizes from ¼ to ½ oz.

(2) Speckles like snappy, flashy spoons in 1/16 to ⅛ oz. in size. Small spinners tipped with a piece of worm also work well, try these in sizes 0-2.

(3) Whitefish will take the smallest baits. Swedish pimples and Mr. Champ in the 1/32 and 1/16 oz. are favourites. Russian type tear drop jigs are also high producers.

(4) Lake herring will at times be caught on larger spoons used for Lake trout, but as a rule, a spoon and pearl combination is the best producer.

(5) Lake trout spoons should be ¼ to 1½ oz. in size. Large flashy spoons with bizzare action work well. Airplane jigs and large home made plugs vertically jigged, produce many trophy lake trout each year.

❀ Twigs to tie your line to work well as quick ice fishing rigs, always choose flexible 2-3′ in length, dogwood and willow being the best branches to use, anchor the stem of the twig close to the hole with ice and snow, wet the base and let it freeze. Make sure the twig is at about 45 degrees over the hole. Add your line to the twig and you're ready to watch it go down as the fish begin to bite.

❀ On extremely cold winter days when snow is constantly being blown in your holes, don't clean it immediately. The snow will work as an insulator and will keep the hole unfrozen for a longer period than just open water.

♣ Many sporting goods stores sell slip-on ice spikes called ice creepers. They're pretty efficient on the ice, helping you to grip your way through the most slippery surfaces.

♣ Floats work well through the ice, watch your float continuously and make sure to break the ice up if it freezes the float on the surface. Using a float is an easy way to change fishing depth and detect the slightest hit even under windy conditions.

♣ A good way to keep your catch alive and fresh until you are done fishing is to cut an extra hole, put your fish on a stringer and drop them through the hole. Tie the stringer to your minnow bucket.

♣ On very windy days, to keep snow from getting in your hole build a wall of snow and water 6″-1′ high on the wind side of the hole, this will make the drifting snow go around the hole.

♣ To make dead minnows look alive use a piece of foil or cardboard and add it to the tip of your twig, as the wind hits these materials it will make the twig go from side to side thus moving the minnow around.

♣ Always take a gaff onto the ice with you. It can be very difficult to land a trophy fish through a hole. With a gaff, reach down and gaff the fish through the lower jaw and gently bring it up through the hole.

♣ Always take an extra pair of gloves or mitts on the ice with you. It's common to get your gloves wet when fighting and landing a fish or working around your hole.

♣ A quick way to warm up your hands when they get really cold is to place them under your arm pits. One way to keep your hands warm on the ice is to make sure you wipe them off every time they get wet.

Ice Fishing

❋ Spring flag tip-ups work well, but make sure the reel spool doesn't get frozen from being left out of the water for long periods of time. Always test the spool before submersing it in the hole.

❋ If you locate a drop-off around a point of land, have your holes placed along its curve with the odd one outside in deeper water. You now have a placement choice if the fish bite shallow or deep.

Fly Fishing

Fly Fishing

There's a special group of anglers who enjoy fishing with an artificial fly or insect. These select anglers spend many hours on rivers, lakes and streams.

With a variety of techniques available to the fly-fisherman, there are still a few facts of importance; a good sense of rhythm, timing and presentation.

If there were ever an opportunity to test your personal fishing skills, it would be fishing with a fly. Unfortunately, fly fishing has had the reputation of being too difficult to master. In contrary, with proper equipment and learned skills, any angler could become successful in fly fishing with just a little practice. Like any other type of fishing, matching the proper tackle is of great importance (rods, reels and line).

Serious fly fisherman study insects and their hatch which helps them to determine what to use. These factors usually apply to casting techniques and a pattern which may convince the most stubborn trout to hit.

Of course fly-fishing can be fun for any species, browns, rainbows, speckies and salmon top the list. From tackle to storage, wet fly to dry fly, this type of fishing is not only an exciting way to fish but it's considered an "art".

Fly Fishing

* When fly-fishing for a particular species, the selection of tackle should reflect the size of the fly, the type and size of water to be fished and the average size of fish in that area.

* Felt or indoor/outdoor carpeting cemented to the sole on waders are not only safer, but they also help you wade quietly allowing you to approach a holding spot without disturbing a potential catch.

* Nylon lines can be left on reel spools from season to season without harm. If any coils develop over winter they can be removed by stretching the line.

* A shock tippet of 40 pound test monofilament will help you land more pike on a fly. Tie a 1 foot section between the leader and the fly.

* Fly fishermen who walk distances or through bush to their favourite fishing spots will find a wading shoe/stocking foot wader particularly nice to use. The waders fold into a package the size of a box of shotgun shells and the boots can be worn like shoes to walk in to the fishing spot. Put the waders on when you get there.

FLY TYER/ROD BUILDER

* If some of your dry flies become so chewed that they no longer float well, just trim it up forming them into a nymph and fish them that way.

✤ When fly-fishing for fish with sharp cutting teeth like the pike, attach a "shock tippet" to the end of your leader. This section of heavy monofilament or light wire prevents the pike's teeth from cutting the fly from the rest of your tackle.

✤ When dry flies don't work during a hatch, a small streamer fly might. Fish try to drive away competitors.

✤ Always match a fly reel with the line weight of the rod. For example, 2 to 4 weight rod - small reel; 4 to 7 weight rod - medium reel; 7 to 12 weight rod - large reel.

✤ Mangled dry flies can be made to look as good as new by a steaming and straightening process.

✤ A clean floating line will get 10 to 20 yards more on each cast over a dirty line.

✤ Use a 12 pound test leader tip when fishing bass in heavy weed cover. You'll need it to pull the bigmouths out to open water.

✤ On sunny days, fish the shady side of the river, right up against the bank. That's usually the place where the trout will hold.

✤ Experienced salmon fly-fishermen almost exclusively use simply hair wing or tube-fly patterns in a very limited range of colours. In fact, a black fly with a small coloured butt is all that is needed to entice the spawning fish to hit.

✤ Don't assume that the largest insect is the one the trout are taking during a multiple hatch. Often the smaller insects of greater numbers is the better choice.

✤ Many fly-fishermen use plastic compartment boxes to house their dry flies. If you affix small strips of magnetic tape to the bottom section, your hooks will hold until they're ready for use.

✤ A stiff monofilament weed guard on a bass bug will let you fish heavily weeded waters. Remember to point the rod at the fly during the slow retrieve.

Fly Fishing

* A strong light leader for sharp-toothed fish is thin piano wire. Available at your local music store.

* Poloroid sun glasses will help spot fish. You'll also be able to see the best areas to cast (underwater cover etc.)

* Wear a belt around the outside of your chest waders. If you fall in by accident, it'll keep most of the water out of your boots.

* If you're planning to use wet or dry flies on a favourite stream or river, hang a piece or strip of flypaper on a tree near the stream for a few hours. On return you should have a pretty good idea of what kind of artificial flies you should use.

* Check the rod guides for chips and rough edges. These can develop and will destroy expensive fly line. Replace the guide when necessary.

* Fly "mud" can be used to sink your line deeper. Apply it to sections of your line that you want to sink fast.

* Entomology is the study of insects. Many anglers tie their flies along a stream when they learn which insect the trout are actually feeding on.

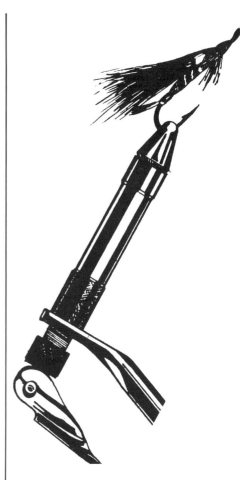

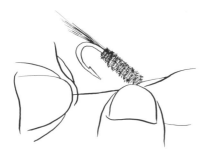

* When tying nymphs, weight some with enough lead to get to the bottom and leave others unleaded to float near the surface.

* When fishing deeper holes and runs with medium sinking fly lines, try adding a length of lead core to the front of your fly line, this will sink your line automatically.

* Carry your camera in a large zip-lock bag. If you walk into the water too far, the camera stays dry and you can still get a few pictures of your trophy trout before going home.

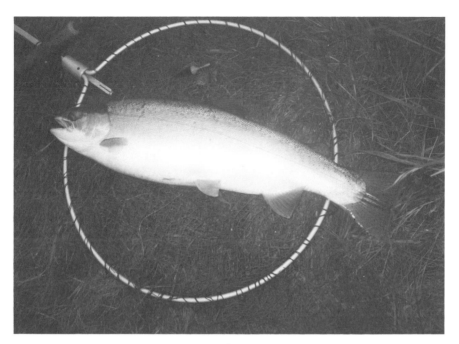

✤ Fly fishermen can take advantage of spring steelhead. Once steelhead finish spawning, they revert back to their bright silver colour and start feeding voraciously. It's at this time that streamers, wet flies and nymphs work well.

✤ Use a short 6 foot leader when fishing big flies in murky water. The fish won't see the leader and the fly will stay close to the strike zone, bottom.

✤ If you want to make your "weighted-forward" sinking fly line, sink even faster by cutting the first few feet off the lead, and tying your leader to the heaviest part of the taper.

✤ Sharpen your hook religiously, if you get several takes but the fish is not hooked, it's time to check it once again.

✤ Wet your monofilament line before you tighten your knots for lubrication and cooling the line.

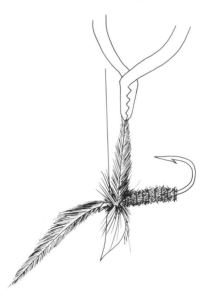

✤ The key elements to a good fly includes silhouette, size, flash, colour and action.

Fly Fishing

* For heavy action fly-fishing such as Atlantic salmon, Pacific salmon and other large fish, the fly reel should have a rim spool. This allows the fisherman to "palm" the reel when he is fighting a large fish. His palm acts as a drag.

* Use a dacron backing on a fly reel so that it doesn't stretch under pressure of fighting a large fish. When wound onto the reel, stretched nylon can spring the reel.

* The key to reading water for all fish, is to locate areas in rivers, lakes or streams where food is concentrated and abundant. In rivers, these locations are the heads of pools and deep runs and in the lakes the points, shoals and drop-offs.

* Fly line "dressing" will aid in making your fly line and leader float much better, especially through fast, rolling water areas.

* Most fly line backing should be changed every few months when used continuously. A fly reel should never be over-filled with backing and line. As a rule of thumb allow a ¼ inch space on your spool to let it function freely without drag.

* To straighten your leader, use a piece of chamois rather than a rubber inner tube. The chamois creates less heat and does not damage the monofilament.

* A stream diary is of utmost importance. In it are kept the notes on daily fishing excursions, the flies, the fish taken, and any other factual data that can provide help on a return trip. Most of all, you'll know which flies need to be tied.

* A sincere thanks to the Izaak Walton Fisherman's Club who provided some of the tips and sketches. Founded in 1971 and has grown to over 325 strong members.

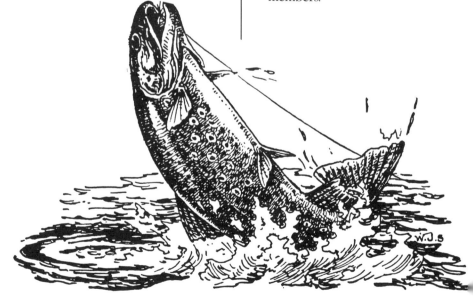

150

Fighting and Landing Fish

Fighting and Landing Fish

Many fishermen hook into a trophy size fish each year, but for one reason or another they seem to lose these fish on a regular basis. Hooking a trophy fish is just the beginning. Knowing how to fight a fish properly is as important as being able to find and hook fish. One of the most important factors in fighting your potential catch is your reel's drag. Many anglers have their drags set improperly or don't use them at all. Other anglers get so excited that they try to land their fish as fast as possible and end up losing them.

A key to successful fishing is knowing your tackle. The angler should not only be familiar with his tackle but he should also be comfortable with it. With these two factors under his belt, confidence will rise during any fight giving him a true advantage over his fish during the battle.

Netting fish should also be mastered. Many fish are fought out and then lost at shore or boat when it's time to net them. Everyone who's spent a particular amount of time fishing from a boat has probably had the disappointing experience of losing a trophy-size fish. Sure, you're bound to lose a few but that's what sportfishing is all about. All in all, there are several important tips that'll aid you in successfully fighting and landing your trophy fish, keeping your losses down to a minimum.

Most importantly there's no better tip than enjoy your fight and release for tomorrow!

Fighting and Landing Fish

❦ Never fight a trophy fish from a boat without lifting a fish stringer and anchor into the boat. The fighting fish will most likely try to go around various lines and even the lower unit of an outboard.

❦ Most people don't realize how important it is to have a good set in a fish. It's not enough just to snap the rod back to set the hook, it is most important to keep lots of tension on the line and crank the reel several times so that the hook point will penetrate beyond the barb.

❦ If you are trying to net a fish that has been hooked on an artificial lure and if it is not hooked deep, always net the fish tail first. This will decrease the chances of getting the hooks caught in the net first. If the fish is hooked deeper in the mouth, head first into the net is fine.

❦ When fighting a fish it's important to hold the rod high in the air, this will maximize the stress you put on the fish by using most of the rod's strength.

❧ Place styrofoam chips in your net handles and even if it flips overboard, it'll float and you can go back and pick it up.

❧ Nets with large plastic strands are better than twine or the linen type. Your net will not only last longer but it'll be easier to get your hooks out after netting.

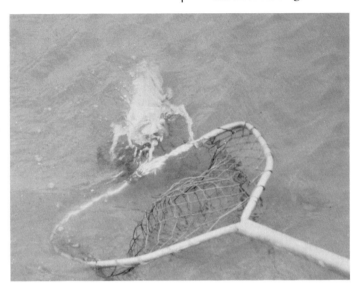

❧ As soon as a large fish is hooked in open water it's a good idea to loosen the drag slightly for the beginning of the fight, as the fish begins to tire tighten the drag to put up more resistance.

❧ When dealing with fish in fast water, lessen the rod pressure allowing the fish to move into your open net. Place the net 2/3 submerged so the current opens the net meshes wide. Make sure it enters head first.

❧ Whenever you get a fish close to the boat, always be ready for that final run. Many fish are lost when people assume they are fought out and won't take any more line out. A fish isn't finished fighting until it's in the boat.

❧ To control a fighting fish in fast water by placing your rod under water and guiding the fish from one side to the other, you can subdue a fish much quicker.

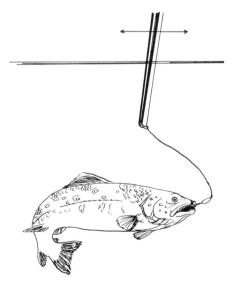

Fighting and Landing Fish

🍁 Landing nets often go under a thrashing and need repair. Use an ordinary bread tie to mend the hole until you can repair it properly.

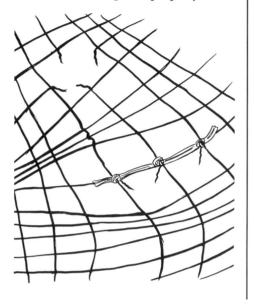

🍁 When fishing in current, always try to get down stream of a fighting fish, this will give you more control over the fish and the odds of the hook being pulled out of its mouth are decreased.

🍁 If you are fighting fish such as bass, musky or trout that jump constantly out of the water, by placing the rod below the water surface when you anticipate a fish jump this will work to keep the fish from making several jumps.

🍁 If you're going to release your fish, don't fight it as long. Try to get it to the boat as quickly as you can and then go through the proper catch and release methods.

✤ Fan casting is the most productive technique whether you're casting from shore, a pier or boat. Don't repeat casts to an area unless you have a follow.

✤ The smoothest drag when fighting a fish is a manual one. By controlling the drag on the line with your fingers you can let the fish take as much or as little as you want it to.

✤ When you're confronted with a jumping fish just push the rod toward the fish creating a controlled slack in the line. As the fish falls back into the water, you can gain control once again. This technique is called "bowing a fish".

✤ Remember, never crank your reel when a fish is running off drag, that's one way your line can get twisted.

✤ When fishing from piers use the countdown method for more strikes.

✤ If a hooked fish wants to run, don't force the fish. Very often when you hesitate and take some of the pressure off the fish it will slow down and stop taking out line.

✤ When fighting bass and other gamefish in heavy cover try to keep the fish's head close to the surface so it can't dive into cover and get caught-up.

Fighting and Landing Fish

✤ Dip the net completely prior to netting your trophy. Enter the whole rim and mesh a few feet from the exhausted fish. Lead the fish into the net, instead of the opposite.

✤ There are key factors in landing a fish after it has been released from your downrigger. Set the hook, keep your rod tip up high don't wind the reel when the fish runs line out, slowly pump your fish with the use of the rod and don't bring your fish by the boat when it's still green.

Live Bait

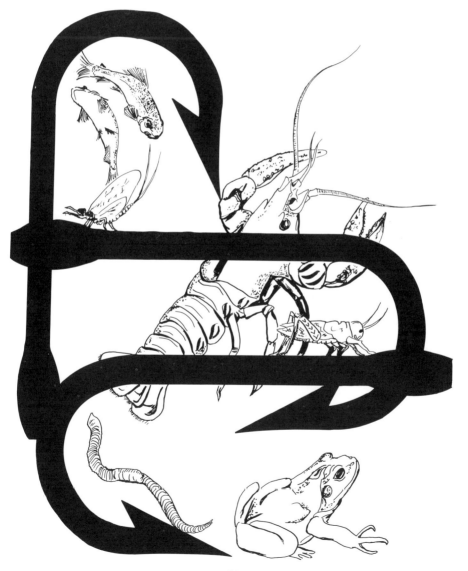

Live Bait

Those fishermen that want to catch walleye consistently will either use worms or minnows. Those who want largemouth bass will usually fish with frogs and those fishing for smallmouth bass will try crayfish, even minnows as bait. Sounds familiar, doesn't it?

Well, one thing for sure there is a significant difference between fishing natural bait and just soaking it. There's one key word that comes to mind and that's "presentation". The offering must be hooked properly and put in front of the fish in a realistic manner.

Many anglers like to go with a lighter line making the bait appear more natural in water. The same goes with terminal tackle such as hooks and weights. The angler needs to go with smallest hook possible unless he's fishing for largemouth bass in deep flipping cover. This change will give him some good hook-setting power to draw the fish out.

At certain times of the year, particular live baits are easier to catch and/or buy. Therefore, most fishermen have a first and second choice that'll help compensate any lack of supply.

However, the following information should help give you some guidelines to catching, preserving and using live bait, no matter what species you're actually fishing for.

Live Bait

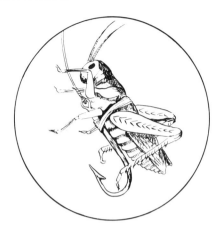

❧ In wooded areas, look for worms under logs and rocks especially after rains. Don't be surprised if you find some salamanders too.

❧ Two or three aspirins in your minnow bucket just may keep your minnows alive until you can change their water.

❧ Keeping dew worms alive, fresh and wriggly is sometimes a problem. Placing a few ice cubes into their bedding during hot weather will indeed keep them fresh. If you can persuade your wife to use the refrigerator between fishing trips, your worms will stay healthy in their container until needed.

❧ To keep insects like grasshoppers alive on your hook longer, don't pierce their body. Just lay them near the hook and wrap a small elastic around their body and hook. They'll be active for a longer time period if the fish are biting.

❧ An excellent bait for trout is water worms (crane fly larvae). If you hook them lightly, they'll flip back and forth in your drift enticing those stubborn trout to bite. Try locating these worms in the mud and sticks of beaver dams.

❧ Even though crayfish live in water, it's not necessary to keep them there while fishing. They will stay alive and fresh in a bait box of moss or even newspaper that has been dampened. Here again, ice cubes will keep them active in warm weather spells.

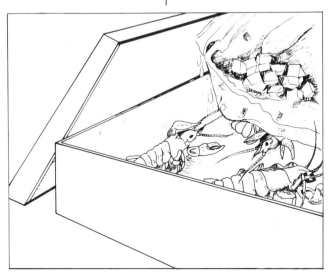

🍁 Leeches can be easily had. Use a large coffee can, place some rocks inside to hold it down and add some fresh fish heads. Put some small slits on each end of the can for the leeches to enter. Sink the can in a pond, marsh or bog. The best time to remove the leeches from the can is before the sun comes up.

🍁 Getting snagged over rocks occurs quite frequently when bait fishing. Add a slip bobber to your line, adjust the depth so that your bait hangs just above the rocks eliminating the snagging problem.

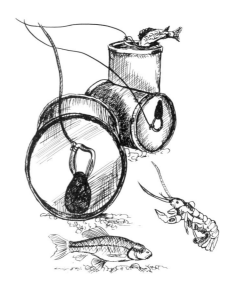

🍁 You can easily catch your bait supply for walleyes and smallmouth by sinking a string of empty beer cans in a weedy river or shallow lake. Minnows, crayfish, even small catfish will hide in these cans. Just go back and lift your trail of cans up for a day's supply of good fishing.

🍁 Many anglers just use crayfish for bass fishing. Yet, small crayfish up to an inch long can make excellent bait for trout. These small crayfish are sometimes hard to locate so just try using the tails of the larger ones. Similar to fishing with worms and other grubs, float them along bottom in deep pools and runs.

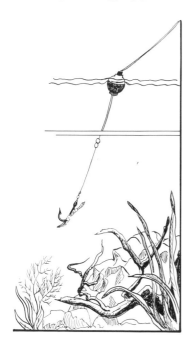

🍁 Most anglers who fish with dew worms have realized that if they put red brick dust in their worm box bedding, that within a few days all the worms will be richer in colour, therefore more attractive to the fish.

🍁 Stinger hooks work great with live bait. Just insert one hook into the head of the bait and the other into the tail. Many fishermen have been using this technique with worms for years. Try stingers hooks on your minnows, salamanders, even frogs when fish are biting short.

Live Bait

courtesy of Plano

🍁 Driving over rough roads can really affect your live bait, especially your worms. Put your bait boxes either on your car seat or boat cushion. Continuous vibrations can affect your worms, even kill them before you get to your fishing spot. Minnows are no different just make sure you have plenty of water in your bucket so that they don't bounce against the sides too much.

🍁 You can make your dew worm float enticingly just off bottom by inflating its body with some air. A hypodermic needle works great. Remember to put just a little air in its head to make it float naturally. Any other place it'll float too vertically.

Live Bait

* Punch several holes in a plastic bag, fill it with ice and tie the top closed. Hang the bag over your bucket. As the ice melts, cool water will drip into the bucket and keep the water from overheating.

* Use a flashlight with red cellophane over the lens when gathering dew worms. The regular white light seems to scare them back into their holes.

* Whenever you are using live bait use as small a hook as possible and minimal terminal tackle as sinkers and leaders. This will make your bait look as natural as possible.

* If a dew worm refuses to be pulled out of the ground, don't force it or it will break. Just apply steady pressure, the worm will tire and eventually slide out of its hole.

* A good time to get your supply of dew worms is after a heavy rain. The worms cover sidewalks and roads in the hundreds. An easy pick-up method is with use of a spatula. When you have enough, just store them in your worm box.

* Old pairs of pantyhose work great for gathering grasshoppers in open fields. Just drag them while walking through at a moderate speed and you eventually have a whole mess of grasshoppers tangled in the nylon. All you have to do is pick them off and place them in your bait bucket.

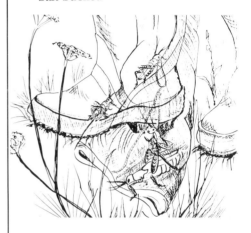

* Keep your live bait fresh and active as possible; use the lightest line possible for the species and conditions; present the bait in a natural manner; stay alert to what's happening; be ready to set the hook, concentration will be your key to success when using live bait.

Live Bait

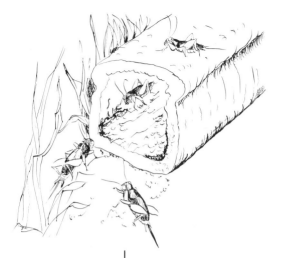

🍁 If you have access to a woodpile, it's possible that you have a decent supply of winter ice fishing bait. Look for some pieces of punky wood and split them. Drilled holes that you locate should host some golden grubs, sometimes as long as ½ inch. Several dozen worms can be located in a short period of time.

🍁 Worms are more productive for fishing if they are not only more active, but also more attractive to the fish. Try scouring your dew worms a few days prior to your fishing trip, place them in some damp moss and they'll get rid of the dirt in their bodies. The result: more translucent and attractive worms.

🍁 Frogs can be easily caught two ways: 1. shine a flashlight directly on them in late evening. This temporarily mesmerizes them. Slowly move in and grab them or better yet, net them. 2. If your reflexes are too slow - use a fly swatter. A light tap will enable you to put them in your bucket and they'll come to, shortly after.

🍁 Terminal tackle in bait fishing is very important. However, remember not to overload your weight. You should be able to feel every nibble. Secondly, allow at least 18″ of length between your bait and your weight. It'll drift in the current more easily and more naturally.

Boating

Boating

Even though boat buying is a gradual thing, it does grow on you. Boat manufacturers have been designing new model boats every year just for the fisherman. It's no wonder that many anglers have been stricken with the so-called "two-foot-itis" disease; trading in their boat for a new one each year.

Most anglers who own boats, big or small, spend at least part of their off-season designing more efficient and productive innerboat set-ups for the upcoming season. Some of these include: rod, lure and accessory storage.

There's no question that if your fishing gear is comfortably placed on your boat, you'll enjoy more productive fishing time on the water. All boats, no matter what their size, need to carry proper safety equipment and should be kept in good operating order. Fishing from boats should be safe as well as fun whether you fish from a canoe, a 14 foot aluminum, an inflatable or even a 33 foot cruiser.

The sharing of hints and tips have helped thousands of boaters in many areas. Therefore, when it comes to boating many factors should be of prime importance: regular maintenance, proper repair, performance, personalized modifications for storage and most of all, the end result "safe fishing fun".

Boating

courtesy of Outboard Marine Corp.

🍁 By cleaning the algae, dirt and grime from your boat's hull several times each season, your performance, speed and fuel efficiency will stay right on track.

🍁 Double check with your insurance company regarding your boat and trailer policy. Make sure you have the proper type of coverage you actually want and need while it is being winterized, left unattended and while it's being trailered.

🍁 Boat keys can be easily lost and ruin your entire fishing trip. Just run the key chain through a hook-eye and screw a cork onto the eye. Floating key chains are also available at most marinas ... cheap too↑

🍁 Microphone clips for your CB or VHF radio are sometimes a bother. Velcro strips work a lot better making the use of your microphone easier to handle and therefore more functional.

🍁 Before leaving home with your boat and trailer make sure the wheel nuts are snug; the trailer is securely tightened to the hitch ball and that the safety lock is installed; safety chains are attached with enough slack; electrical system is hooked up and working properly; tie-downs are tight; winch is locked and that your vehicle's mirrors are adjusted correctly for proper visibility.

When you're going into a back lake to do some fishing in solitude, a anchor for your canoe will probably come in handy. To avoid carrying one in, just fold up an onion bag in your knapsack. When you arrive at your favourite lake, just place a rock into the bag and attach it to your canoe.

By placing some one inch thick sheets of styrofoam in an unused storage box on your boat can easily make it into an excellent ice chest. Just glue the pieces with RTV silicone into place leaving the drain plug uncovered for proper drainage.

Remember port is left and starboard is right, follow proper boating regulations, be alert to weather conditions and information at all times.

If your boat has a top, by all means put it up when you're spending a number of hours fishing on the lake. You can never get enough protection from the damaging rays of the sun.

When it comes to launching a boat there are a number of guidelines one needs to be aware of: always check your ramp site; double check that your drain plug is securely in placc, your trailcr lights should bc disconnected; trim your motor into the up position; make sure your bow and stern lines are accessible; always back your boat up slowly.

Purchasing a motor over 10 hp may not necessarily be the right way to go. Don't forget, you're going to have to load this heavier motor onto your boat, carry it certain distances and also have it registered. In almost every case, a 5 to 9.9 hp will more than do the job for your 12 to 16′ aluminum.

Boating

Courtesy of Regal Boats of Canada

🍁 A good boater should use courtesy, common sense, and safety at all times.

🍁 Carrying a boat on top of your car can sometimes cause problems. For instance, the ropes holding the boat at the front and back may rub the paint finish off your car. You can prevent this by placing foam rubber pads where the rope touches the car. The rubber can be held in place by taping the pieces to the rope.

🍁 Crossing a fast moving stream with a canoe can sometimes be a problem. Just angle your craft a few degrees towards the other shore but upstream. By using this technique, you'll prevent the current from taking you and your canoe a long distance downstream.

🍁 The best prevention for mildew is ventilation. Careful drying and cleaning of all surfaces and fabrics after each trip is a must to insure prevention of mildew.

🍁 Keep some spare clothing in a watertight plastic bag along with a flashlight, whistle, knife, first-aid kit even emergency rations if possible.

🍁 If you own a boat shed or garage, hang a tennis ball from the ceiling about 3 feet off the wall, low enough so that it bounces off the boat when you back in. This will not only protect your propeller and trailer lights but it'll also protect the back of your garage.

🍁 Over the years, more and more anglers have turned to using hydrographical maps. Much available information can be obtained like: variable water depths, weed lines, shoals etc. These can be purchased quite reasonably from the Canada Map Office, 615 Booth Street, Ottawa, Ontario. K1A 0E9.

🍁 Here's a handy formula for estimating hull speed. An important piece of information for tournament fishermen travelling from one spot to another as well as anglers interested in the maximum miles per hour that their outboard can efficiently move the hull. Just multiply 1.3 times the square root of the waterline length in feet.

🍁 It is essential to maintain the tire manufacturers recommended pressure for your trailer tires. Too soft a tire will overheat and could cause a blowout. Too hard a tire, although not dangerous, causes a rough ride.

🍁 There are many ways to protect your boating and hydrographical maps, here's one. Cover the surfaces with a transparent contact sheeting. These plastic materials are self-adhesive and can be purchased in most department or hardware stores. For more protection, keep the maps rolled up in PVC pipe at home with both ends capped. Even old golf tubes will do.

🍁 Trim your outboard out if the bow is too low and it bangs into oncoming waves. Trim your outboard in if your bow is too high and causes porpoising.

🍁 Most fishing specialists say that it's alright to sing and shout but never toss an anchor or drop heavy objects inside your boat.

courtesy of Outboard Marine Corp.

173

Boating

courtesy of Outboard Marine Corp.

🍁 Make sure you mix your gasoline and oil as recommended by your manufacturer. You'll find that it'll run smoother, start easier and have a longer life.

🍁 If you stringer your fish, hang them from the forward part of your boat. Like many anglers who forget when travelling from spot to spot, you'll see your catch flopping quicker and they won't become tangled in the prop.

🍁 Every year more and more fishermen have realized the importance of electric outboards. They're ideal for fishing shallow waters, offer great control over weed lines and are super efficient and quiet.

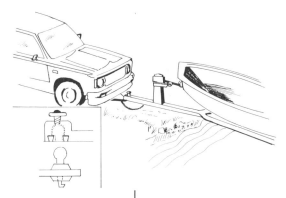

🍁 If you're constantly having trouble landing your boat from a trailer. Install a ball hitch on your vehicle's front bumper. When you get to the ramp site, unhitch the trailer from its regular position and attach it to the front. You'll gain more control and better vision. When you're finished fishing, just pick up your boat in the same manner, switching the trailer before your trip home.

🍁 Don't pile all your items into the stern of your boat when trailering. It may lift your hitch and cause steering problems especially on the highway.

🍁 A handy item on any boat is a marker buoy. When you want to mark a hot fishing hole or the spot where you dropped something overboard, all you have to do is to heave your marker overboard. The simplest kind of marker can be made from a screw-top plastic jug with about 25 feet of line wrapped around it with a heavy sinker.

🍁 If you want a super looking boat finish, use furniture polish in the spray can. The dirt and grim will just float off with a spray from your water hose.

❧ Many small boat owners have their boats poorly equipped when it comes to safety. The minimum requirements that should be carried on your boat when fishing should consist of: a first-aid kit, flares, a flashlight, knife, tool kit, waterproof matches and a lifejacket for everyone aboard.

❧ When night fishing in a boat, reflector tape strips placed on hard to find items will help you locate them quicker. Here are some suggestions: tackle boxes, net handles, gaffs etc.

❧ Canoes should not be used for fishing unless you are an experienced canoeist. These crafts can be dangerous in the hands of the inexperienced.

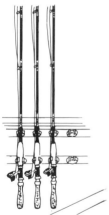

❧ Fishing gear such as your rods and reels can get pretty beat-up when bounced around in a boat. Hardware departments carry clips for broom handles etc. These same clips can be attached to your boat so that your rods stand up evenly while the boat is running to your next fishing spot.

❤ Many accidents occur every year in boats both big and small. These tips can save your life:

1. Don't wander too far in big waters if you're in a small boat.

2. Any drastic changes in weather can be harmful to everyone in the boat – take all necessary precautions in inclement weather.

3. Make sure that your boat is safety equipped according to its size.

4. Make sure everyone aboard is wearing life jackets.

5. Watch your alcohol intake not only when fishing but when it comes to operating a boat, abstain.

Courtesy of Regal Boats of Canada

❤ Many anglers make their own boat anchors. Check at your local truck service centre or auto parts specialty house for a broken truck axle shaft. All you have to do is weld a big nut onto the end of the shaft and you've got yourself an 8 lb. anchor.

❤ Under all boating conditions, rough water and/or stormy, stay calm. If by chance you're dumped out of a canoe in heavy rapids, get upstream on the canoe if possible, so that the canoe can't ram you. When floating downstream, try to go feet first so that you can see where the current is and other obstructions like rocks and boulders.

Boating

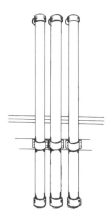

🍁 Boat rod holders can be easily made from plastic PVC pipe. With various modifications, the pieces can adapt and make great holders on any boat.

🍁 Always wear an approved life jacket when in a travelling boat and if you profess to be a stand-up fisherman, make sure your life jacket remains on. Set a good example especially for the younger ones.

🍁 The worst item to use to cover your outboard motor over the winter is a plastic sheet. It will not only hold moisture, but it can scratch your paint finish. Use an old sheet or large cloth to keep the dust out and the fresh air in.

🍁 There's all kinds of home-made anchors to be made. A cheap, quiet yet durable one can be made from the use of a plastic bleach bottle. Just fill it with sand or concrete mix, screw the cap back on and attach an anchor rope through it's handle and it's ready for use.

🍁 Never stand directly in front of a trailer winch line when cranking a boat into position. A parting rope or cable could catapult backwards or a handle could spin causing serious injury.

⚜ Make sure you remove all weeds clinging to your boat, outboard motor or trailer when travelling from one spot to another. This conservation practice will help prevent undesirable weeds being introduced to other Canadian waters.

⚜ When you need a marker at the spur-of-the-moment, a bumper cushion will work just great. By adding a weight on one end will enable one end to stand up and even be more visible.

⚜ Small squares of sample carpeting are available dirt-cheap from most rug centres. They can be used to deaden noise, especially in aluminum boats. You can place them under tackle boxes, ice chests, gas tanks even in anchor storage areas.

⚜ A sea anchor or even a plastic bucket will help troll-down the speed of your boat. Many times your boat travels just a little too fast for a particular species to hit. Dropping your home-made sea-anchor back about 10 feet may just do the trick.

⚜ Here's a way to keep your map open for viewing and protected while on your boat. By having some available dash, just place your map flat and along each side just place two long strips of velcro. Purchase a piece of plexiglass covering the entire map. Two matching velcro straps on the plexiglass will hold it in place and protected until it's time to change maps.

⚜ You can easily ruin your canoe paddle by pushing off docks, shallow water and rocks. Just use the other end which is more blunt and can take this type of beating. By doing this, your paddle will serve you better and longer.

Boating

courtesy of Outboard Marine Corp.

❧ The length of your boat is as important as its beam. One of the key characteristics missing in most boats is a good-sized cockpit. Added length will help provide this feature.

Safety and First Aid

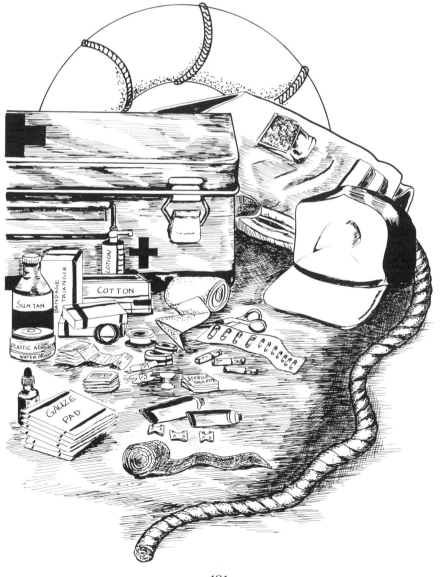

Safety and First-Aid

Whether you consider yourself an amateur or a professional, safety and first-aid should be learned and learned well. All anglers, young and old should practice and also instruct others to promote safety in sportfishing. Like the boy scouts motto "be prepared"; you never know when you will need to administer first aid.

You could be wading in a river or fishing in a boat when an accident or first-aid situation may occurr. It's here where the fisherman will need to use discretion and caution no matter what the circumstance.

Each year, anglers suffer injuries even die, due to negligence and/or poor discipline. Seasonal fishing has its advantages and disadvantages. Therefore, being abreast of weather conditions, alert to possible accident situations, as well as uderstanding the basics of first-aid, safety may at some point, even save a life.

♣ Many would-be fishermen drown each year from boating accidents and hundreds more are saved. If you're a below average swimmer, rescuing individuals need a little instruction. Try to use a fishing rod, paddle, a rope, or even your jacket to reach him. When he grabs on, pull him in, You can always use another boat to get to him when he's too far to reach from shore.

♣ While travelling to your fishing spot, it's wise to remove your lures/hooks from your rod. This is not only a good safety measure, but you won't have to spend time removing hooks out of your upholstery when you arrive.

♣ Many boats have exploded during the fueling process. Remember to shut off the engine(s) and any other electrical device capable of producing a spark; close all hatches, windows etc. so that the fumes can't blow aboard; all passengers should be ashore and away from the gas tanks; without question, no smoking within the fueling area; all portable fuel tanks should be removed from the boat and filled on shore.

♣ Many fishermen travel hundreds of miles each year to reach their fishing hot spot. Unfortunately, some anglers get involved in auto accidents due to the high concentration of summer traffic. Remember to take the following steps immediately:

1. Warn oncoming vehicles of the accident by either using flares or have a helper flag down oncoming traffic.

2. Get a call in for help as soon as possible.

3. Anyone hurt should be treated immediately.

4. If fire threatens, move all passengers to a safe area.

♣ Stinging insects are bothersome throughout the fishing season. If you do get stung, you can help the situation by removing the stinger if there is one. Apply a paste of baking soda on ant and bee stings, lemon juice or vinegar on stings from wasps. Bites from insects such as mosquitos and blackflies can be soothed by applying calamine lotion.

✤ A bailing can should be aboard every type of boat. You never know when your automatic or manual bridge pump may break down. It's nothing to make up a couple of bailers from a plastic bleach bottle. Just cut out the bottom part into a scoop effect. Leave the cap on and your moulded handle will do the rest.

✤ Batteries in all flashlights should be checked monthly before every trip. If an emergency occurs, it would be a shame if the batteries went dead for some reason.

✤ To remove an embedded hook, attach a loop to the hook bend. Lightly depress the hook with your thumb, sharply jerk on the cord loop to remove hook.

✤ While fishing, many anglers, sunworshippers or not, forget about the damage the sun can perform on their skin. The best solution is to use the proper sunscreen before the sun can do its trick. (Numbers 5 to 10 are fairly protective). Don't overdo it, it's better to gradually tan than to take a beating the first couple of days. Wear a wide brimmed hat or cap and if you're spending a long day on the water, it would be wise to wear a long light coloured shirt as well. At the end of the day, a skin moisturizer should be used.

✤ Even pro fishermen accidently hook themselves through the flesh. Sometimes immediate help cannot be reached. These procedures will help you remove most hooks. Using a sterilized blunt needle, run the needle down the path of the hook and rotate it until it's on the barb side of the hook. Back out the hook using the end of the needle as support. Back out the needle, then dab the wound with an antibiotic solution. Place a bandage over the cut to prevent any infection.

press lightly

sharp jerk

Safety and First Aid

✤ If by chance you get a slight burn from a campfire or finger contact on a spooling reel, apply cold water or ice for 10 minutes or so. A burn ointment or a baking soda paste should be applied under a light bandage.

✤ Be alert to rising waters if you have to make a trip back across the stream. Heavy rains and tides can change water depths even up to 3 feet.

✤ Be careful when crossing obstructions like fences. Try to cross them near stiles using extreme care especially when you're wearing waders and carrying your fishing equipment. A simple task may result in an unfortunate accident or even something as simple as puncturing your waders.

✤ Know and obey the rules of the road afloat. Operate with not only care and courtesy to boaters and fishermen, but also with common sense.

✤ If you pierce your fingertips or palm with a fishing hook or from a fish, make sure you apply pressure to the puncture to promote some bleeding. This technique will help discharge any material that may cause infection.

✤ To help prevent insect bites, wear light-coloured clothing, long-sleeved shirts and pants and a good insect repellent. Be careful when applying different solutions and sprays, especially when dealing with the face, eyes, and mouth.

✤ Whether fishing along or with your fishing buddy, be careful when you cast. You never know when a back-whip action could hook someone. A double check behind or beside you, could prevent an accident from occurring.

Cleaning
and
Cooking

Cleaning and Cooking Fish

Even though each type of fish has an individual flavour, texture and appearance; the basic rules for cleaning and cooking fish are easy to follow.

Of course there are many guidelines to keeping your catch fresh as well as preserving your fillets, steaks or whole fish. True, filleting is by far the most popular and most common method of cleaning your catch, and with a little practice and some knowledge from the following tips, anyone can master the technique.

If you plan to do alot of fishing and you enjoy eating fish, it's important to take steps to make sure your catch will taste as fresh as possible at the table, Many anglers use rough cleaning methods before storing their fish which takes some of the flavour out of the fish and leaves many broken bones inside the fish which becomes a nuisance when you are eating your meal. From panfrying to microwaving, care must be taken with each freshwater species you catch.

Sportfishing is enjoyable and relaxing - your dinner can be too! Pay heed to these hints and techniques and you'll increase your enjoyment of catching and preparing your fish properly.

Cleaning and Cooking

✦ Normark has a filleting glove out on the market to help you clean spiny fish like bass and panfish. The glove is also worn to help prevent cuts to your skin while cleaning.

✦ Always trim the fatty tissue around the bellies of fish before cooking them. This will give you a tastier fish to eat.

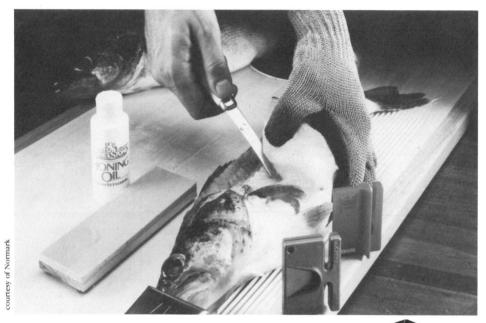

courtesy of Normark

✦ Many anglers like to camp and fish in back lakes. An easily-made skillet is better than hauling one. Bend a wire coat hanger into a circle with a handle formation. Cover the entire circle with a double layer or aluminum foil, crimping it over the edges to make your disposable and workable frying pan.

✦ Fish are usually cut in fillet or steaks for cooking. Try oven cooking whole large fish in foil paper. Add onions and fresh parsley to take any undesirable flavour away.

Cleaning and Cooking

🍁 When you clean your catch, instead of tossing the remains into the garbage can, bury the remains around your bushes and flowers for free fertilizer. Not only will your flowers smell sweeter, but so will your garbage.

🍁 Fish caught in warm, weedy mud-bottomed lakes will taste better if they are skinned, whereas fish caught in cold, clear water are fine if they are just scaled for eating.

🍁 To kill the odour left on your hands after cleaning fish, wash then with salt. The second time through, just lather them up and wipe away the soap suds with a dry towel.

🍁 Whenever cooking fish over a fire, make a fire that is small, but which burns hot. Don't use wet wood or green wood that will create a lot of smoke.

🍁 Fish should be cleaned as soon as possible and kept cool either on ice or frozen.

🍁 If you are on a backpacking or canoe trip and would like to keep fish to take home, don't kill them right away. Try to keep them alive on a stringer in the water and only kill them just before going home.

🍁 In order to preserve the flavour of your catch, clean your fish as soon as possible.

🍁 Here are some guidelines in keeping your catch fresh; slime and/or scale the fish as soon as possible; immediately bleed the fish (cut the fish behind the gills on the underneath side); remove the intestines. The digestive enzymes of feeding fish are so active that they'll continue their activity and begin to digest the fish itself; remove the dark streak along the backbone (the kidney), cut the covering membrance and scrape it out with a spoon. It also is a chief source of flavour destroying enzymes. Removing the head will save some cooler and freezer space.

Cleaning and Cooking

1. Make first cut just behind the gills. Slice down to the bone, then, without removing blade, turn it and slice straight along backbone...

2. ... to the tail. Note that the fillet has been cut away from the rest of the fish. After slicing fillet off at tail, turn fish over and repeat procedure on the other side.

3. With both sides removed, you have cut away both fillets without disturbing fish's entrails. This is the neatest and fastest way to prepare fish. Now to finish the fillets ...

4. Next step is to remove the rib section. Again, a sharp, flexible knife is important to avoid wasting meat. Insert blade close to rib bones and slice entire section away. This should be done before skin is removed to keep waste to a minimum.

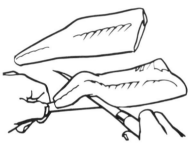

5. Removing the skin from each fillet is simply a matter of inserting the knife at the tail and "cutting" the meat from the skin. Start cut ½ inch from tail end of skin, allowing wedge for best grip. With the proper knife, like the "Fish 'N Fillet," it's easily done.

6. Here is each fillet, ready for the pan, or freezer. Note there is no waste. Remember not to overwash fillets. This will preserve tasty juices and keep meat in its firm natural state.

Cleaning and Cooking

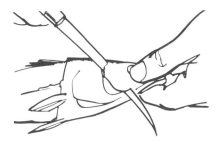

7. Cutting out the "cheeks" is the next important step. Few fishermen know that cheeks are the filet mignon of the fish. Though small, they're tasty and well worth saving.

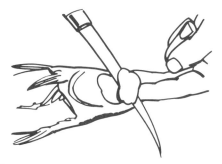

8. Slice into cheek where indicated then "scoop out" meat with blade, peeling away skin. Repeat on the other side. Many fishermen save cheeks until they have accumulated enough for a real gourmet's delight.

9. Here are all parts of the fish after you've finished. Note fish head, entrails, spine, tail and fins stay intact. This is the neatest way to prepare most game fish and, once you've mastered these few steps, the easiest.

🍁 Never leave fresh fish soaking in water. Wash fish quickly, drain and dry carefully. Don't overcook your catch and turn only once during cooking.

🍁 An excellent method for cooking fish is barbecuing. Both steaks and fillets can be cooked in this manner. Don't forget to dab the fish with paper towels and place the fish onto double foil pads, cut to size on your grill. Baste frequently with a lemon/butter mixture and test with a fork until it flakes.

🍁 Particular gamefish like largemouth bass and pike have a strong tasting flesh in the lateral line. This dark coloured flesh along the side of a fish should be removed if you plan to freeze your catch for more than one month.

courtesy of Normark

Cleaning and Cooking

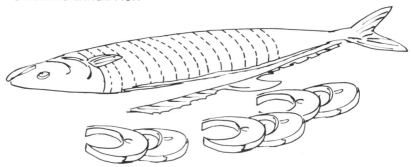

courtesy of Normark

Cut steak 3/4 to 1½ inches thick at right angles to back bone of fish.

✤ A good rule of thumb when it comes to steaking fish is 1. fish over 6 pounds can be steaked, yet fish over 10 pounds should be steaked or chunked, so they are easier to cook. Remember to trim and throw away the fatty belly of the steak ends.

✤ The best way to refrigerate fish is to wipe your catch (fillets, whole fish or steaks) with paper towels; place them on paper towels; cover them tightly with a stretch plastic wrap and they're ready to get chilled.

✤ An easy way to check your fish to see if it is thoroughly cooked when panfrying, is to insert the fork at the backbone section and twist. The flesh will separate easily from the bone when done.

✤ The most productive way to keep your catch fresh is to place them in a cooler that is filled to the brim with cracked or crushed ice.

✤ There's nothing like a shore lunch. Even when your catch is too small for filleting, it'll be just right for pan-frying. Just clean the cavity leaving the head, fins, and tail, wipe each fish with a dry paper towel, roll them in flour and seasoning and you're ready to go. Melt a little butter over a medium hot fire, and your fish will brown beautifully in 6 to 10 minutes.

✤ By using a log or board with a knife, nail or another sharp object, you can easily fillet or scale your catch without having it slip and move around.

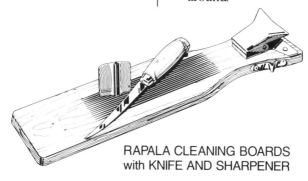

RAPALA CLEANING BOARDS
with KNIFE AND SHARPENER

♣ To get a tasty fried fish, always sear the outside on high heat. This will help to hold some moisture and most of the flavour in the flesh as it is cooking.

♣ Many anglers and their wives have turned to microwave cooking. Remember, lean fish should be microwaved at 100% power and oily fish at 50%. Fattier fish tend to pop (their meat separates) at higher settings.

♣ If you aren't sure if the fish you have caught is spoiled or not, from being out too much, check its ribs. If the ribs detach themselves from the flesh, the fish is starting to spoil.

♣ Whether you're thawing whole or cut fillets, place the fish in a shallow pan and pour enough fresh milk to cover the fish completely. Most folks who use this method say, "the milk seems to restore its fresh caught flavour".

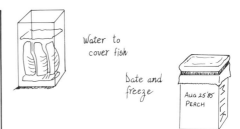

Water to cover fish

Date and freeze

Aug 25 '85
PERCH

♣ Thoroughly washed milk cartons make an excellent container for freezing your catch. Just make sure your fish are carefully covered by water, date and place a piece of foil on top before freezing.

♣ The flesh of fish carries many tasty juices, much like that of good meat. Remember to wash your fillets in cold water and with as little force as possible. This will help to keep these juices in.

♣ Many scissors like the ones from Normark Industries are specially designed to help clean your catch. They're ideal for gilling and gutting trout in the field and for the cleaning of other small fish such as smelt and perch.

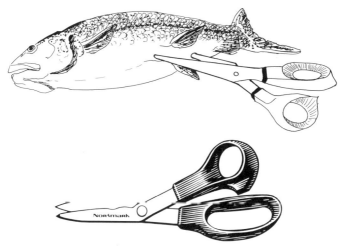

GAME, FISH & FOWL SHEARS

Cleaning and Cooking

NEWLY DESIGNED SPOON FILLET KNIFE AND FOLDING
FILLET KNIFE BY NORMARK

❀ Instead of buying ice for storing your fish, freeze large blocks of ice at home. Take milk bags that don't leak, fill them with water, seal them and freeze them. Put 6-8 in your cooler and they will keep for one to two days.

❀ To remove any strong taste from various fish, let the fish soak in beaten eggs in a bowl. The longer the fish is allowed to soak the milder it will taste.

❀ When filleting walleye, cut out the cheeks and fry them, many people consider them a "gourmet delight" After being fried they taste like scallops.

❀ Fish spoil quickly without air circulation so prevent using non-porous wrapping such as plastic garbage bags for holding fish for a period of time. Ice coolers, most burlap bags and newspapers are better.

❀ Never transport fish in the trunk of a car of a back seat. Always take a cooler with you and some ice and gut the fish as soon as you catch it.

Your Fishing Tips, Hints and Techniques

Your Fishing Tips, Hints and Techniques

Convenient Order Form

I would like to have additional copies of this book.

"CANADIAN SPORTFISHING"

An illustrated handbook of over
1000 fishing tips, hints and techniques.

Please mail me_____copies to the address below:

Name _____

Address _____

_____

IRWIN
PUBLISHING INC.
180 West Beaver Creek Road
Richmond Hill, Ontario L4B 1B4

ostage, tax and

rmation).